GW00601870

IAN FINLAY

THE CENTRAL HIGHLANDS

B. T. Batsford Ltd.
London

First published 1976

Text copyright Ian Finlay 1976

ISBN 0 7134 3132 6

Computer typeset by Input Typesetting Ltd,
4 Valentine Place, London SE1
Made and printed by
Biddles of Guildford, Surrey
for the publishers B. T. Batsford Ltd. 4 Fitzhardinge Street,
London W1H 0AH

CONTENTS

MR. M. TEADHAM
KT4 7EX
SUBJECT........*A*
NUMBER........333

Acknowledgements

The Author and Publishers would like to thank the following for the photographs reproduced in this book: the British Council, no. 15; the Rt. Hon. the Earl Cawdor, no. 22; Anthony Finlay, nos. 7, 8; the National Galleries of Scotland, no. 14; the National Trust for Scotland, nos. 9, 11, 12, 20, 21; the Royal Scottish Museum, no. 2; D. C. Thomson & Co, no. 16.

No. 24 is Crown Copyright, reproduced by permission of the Controller of H. M. Stationery Office, and nos. 1, 3, 4, 5, 6, 10, 13, 18, 19, 23 are by the Author.

Illustrations

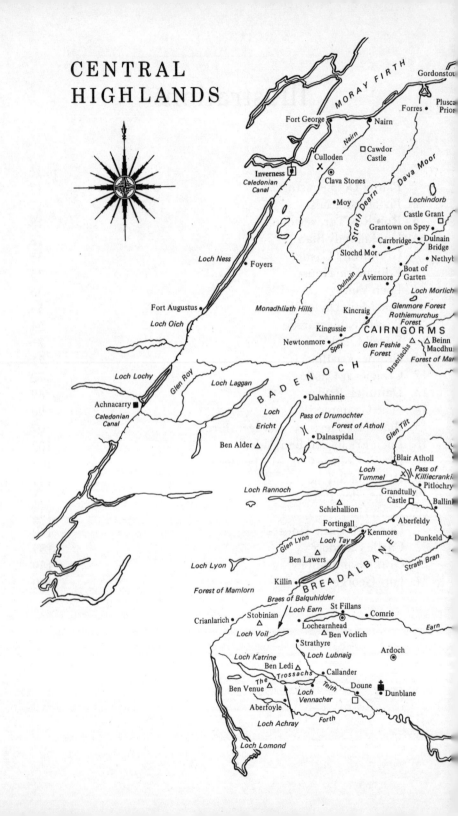

⊙ Spynie Palace
Elgin
• Fochabers

BUCHAN

lothes •
Craigellachie
• Keith
Deveron
• Turriff
• New Deer

• Dufftown
☐ ■✝ Forgue Church
Wells of
Ythan
Fyvie
☐ Castle

llindalloch
astle
S T R A T H B O G I E
Huntly

Ellon

mintoul

■ Leith Hall
Insch •

✝ Chapel of Garioch
✗ Harlaw

Kildrummy
Castle ☐
Castle Fraser ☐ △
Alford
■ Bennachie ⊙ • Inverurie

Don
Monymusk

Craigievar Castle ☐
☐ Midmar Castle

■ ■ ABERDEEN

Aboyne
Kincardine
• O' Neil
Ballater
Dee
☐ Crathes Castle
Banchory

☐ Balmoral Castle
T H E   M O U N T H

emar
△
Lochnagar

Tarfside
• Cairn O' Mounth

Howe of the Mearns
Fettercairn •
• Laurencekirk

Edzell ☐
N. Esk

l's
ow

Glen Clova

Glen Prosen

Brechin ✝
☐
• Montrose

Cortachy
Castle ᘐ☐
S. Esk

Kirriemuir •
⊙ Aberlemno

Alyth
• **Forfar**

irgowrie
☐
⊙ Glamis

STRATHMORE
Meigle

ᘐuthil
Coupar
Angus
Sidlaw Hills

• **Arbroath**

DUNDEE
☐

FIRTH
OF TAY

ERTH
Carse of Gowrie

N O R T H

S E A

△ *mountain or hill*

■ *mansion*

☐ *castle*

✝ *church*

⊙ *archaeological site*
   or ancient monument

✗ *battlefield*

0   5   10   20 ┐ miles
├──────┼──────┼──────────────┤ km
       10   20   30

For Veronica

Introduction

Some readers may prefer to leapfrog this Introduction and proceed to the chapters which follow; but to my mind this would be a pity, because no part of the Highlands is a mere playground for tourist or angler or climber any more, and the new problems of the area are as worthy of everyone's attention as the scenery or history or archaeology, and some people may find them of compelling interest. I respect the recent writer on the Highlands who sweeps aside most modern literature about the area as 'cauld kale het again', a jibe only too well deserved. At the same time I think that the great and absorbing problems which, for good or ill, are changing much of the traditional scene should be dealt with early in a book of this kind and not piecemeal later, not merely because they might intrude on some pleasant jaunts but because they raise issues so fundamental that they deserve to be brought into the forefront where the reader may decide whether he will take them with him through to the end of the book or, if he so chooses, dodge them.

This book is about the Central Highlands, a specific area. Both romantics and realists in recent times have tended to regard the Highlands as meaning the *Gaidhealtachd,* the area west and north-west of the Great Glen where Gaelic is or was until fairly recently widely spoken. Indeed, one book on what is to become of the Highlands, so far as cultural and economic questions are concerned, devotes itself wholly to the Crofter Counties, two of which have nothing to do with the Highlands by any definition. In a sense therefore the Central Highlands are a little neglected. They are so far past a renaissance of Gaelic culture and language that those who strive for this aim probably consider them lost, and then again the challenge of North Sea Oil and its related industries is of very little direct concern to them. Yet in many respects the central area, like the Highlands in total, is at a cross-roads. It is not easy to choose the right way ahead. There is still a strong conservative lobby ready to grasp the fiery cross over any threat to traditional ways, and at the other extreme there are aggressive progressives who believe in exploiting a long-neglected wilderness by dragging it into the rat-race of the materialism which threatens the future of all of us. There are questions within questions here, fascinating if they were not so agonising. Whose interest is to prevail – the Highlander's, or Britain's as an entirety? What is the Highlander's true interest? In the long term, is his interest not also Britain's? Anyone who knows the history of the Highlands knows what the answer has been in the past. The 'Highland haemophilia' to which I referred in the first book I ever wrote is as hard to eradicate as the other sort. Now some are glimpsing bigger profits among those hills than were ever brought in by deer or sheep, and the money is already flowing south. At the same time the trickle of urban refugees, the white settlers, is flowing faster and yet faster in the opposite direction and a new scale of values is driving natives from the glens. The Highlands need a few men of stature to arise in their wisdom. It is not enough to ask for Cuchulainn and be given a Committee.

I have written elsewhere that the Highlands as an entity are a creation not so much of the upheavals of Nature as of the Victorians. This is even more true of the Central Highlands. Nature certainly wrought a great range of mountains there, as usual afterwards doing her best to wear down and erode what she had heaved up. The result, until comparatively recent times, was a complex of high ridges and deep glens, of torrents and bogs, which were refuges for many sorts of wild animals and for men equally untameable. In one way the Central Highlands were more inaccessible than the Western Highlands, because seaways penetrated most of the west, and we know that Pictish, and later Viking fleets were constantly busy on those seaways. Agricola and his legions got within sight at least of the Moray Firth, but he could only achieve this by skirting the mountains and there is no evidence that he ever tried to push deeply into them. This mountain mass came to be called the Grampians, an erroneous name based on a classical author's mistake, but now sanctified by long usage. In subjugating this wilderness the early Stewart kings had some success, and Edward I led a big army into the most unlikely places although it was no conquest and his enemies usually reoccupied at once whatever ground his tents had covered. General Wade was the first man to hold down any considerable part of this country, which he did by building a system of military roads and forts, but they did little to halt the Jacobite clans when Charles Edward rallied them. The Butcher Cumberland made a desert and called it peace, but the glens still festered with resentment while the clans, disarmed and unkilted, felt in nearly empty purses for money to send to their chiefs in exile. Not until Victoria arrived and fell in love with the Highlands – in the first place because they looked like Thuringia! – did the taming process really begin. Where the Hanoverians had made the mistake of proscribing these outlandish people and their customs, the Victorians came to foster them, after their fashion. In a generation or two they had turned the Grampian area into a sort of precursor of the national parks, although not of course a park for just anyone who chose to come. Following princely example Victorian society took over the tartan, and it became the thing to have a Highland grandmother.

The Central Highlands are easily defined. There is nothing arbitrary about their boundaries. The Highland fault line divides them from the low lands to the south, and the Great Glen separates them dramatically from the north-western area. The Moor of Rannoch is perhaps a rather more vague frontier to the west. The least satisfactory outline is on the east and north, and it may seem odd if I include some of the Carse of Gowrie and of Strathmore, still more part of the wide, flat lands of the Laigh of Moray, but historically those areas are closely bound to the hill-country which fringes them. It may seem odd, too, to touch on Aberdeen, but not on Dundee or other east-coast towns, but Dundee turns its back on the Grampians in ways which Aberdeen does not. Physically, then, the Central Highlands are distinct. Climatically too they are quite different from the rest of the Highlands.

The main strike of the rocks in this great Grampian region is north-east and south-west. They are some of the most ancient in the British Isles, results of a process which geologists sometimes call the Caledonian orogenesis. One feature of this rugged landscape will impress anyone looking at it from a vantage-point such as Stirling Castle. Tumbled as this horizon of high tops is, there are really no dominant peaks soaring far above their fellows. There is a levelling off or crushing down effect, almost as if some enormous plane had been at work, and this in fact is true, for the levelling is the work of glaciers in successive ice ages. Those mountains are relics of a range which may have rivalled any on earth. On closer inspection many of them seem worn stumps, rounded in outline, with only here and there something more shapely or dramatic, where an iron-hard boss of quartzite has produced a peak such as Schiehallion or Ben-y-ghlo, or where metamorphic grits have endured, as with Ben Ledi or Ben Vorlich. One has to get among those hills, perhaps even climb them, to find out how formidable they can be. The glens dividing them and the moorlands between may themselves impose a weary trudge of many miles through bog and tarn, and at all seasons save perhaps high summer the loftier plateaux are liable to become suddenly grim sub-arctic wastes. It is not hard to understand why for so many centuries invaders had considerable respect for those hills. As to the directional strike, the main features are two: the great wall of hills visible from the central Lowlands to Angus, and the Great Glen which, flooded by Loch Ness and Loch Lochy, cut off the Central Highlands from the north-west. Both result from gigantic faults. The first has been called one of the finest examples of a fault scarp to be found anywhere, towering as it does above a valley excavated in the Old Red Sandstone. In the case of the Great Glen, some suppose there has been a sideways thrust of the rock masses along this line. Among the few routes which penetrate directly through the general diagonal strike of the region is that which carries the Great North Road from Perth up over the Drumochter Pass, after which it follows the strike down by way of the head-waters of the Spey, to deviate again at Carrbridge and carry the road across the Slochd summit to Inverness.

The people who live here in this central region are as different from those who live in the west and north as the landscapes are different. That fusion of Celt and Norse which, in varying degrees, is so apparent in west and north, in the Central Highlands is much less marked and is modified by big infusions of other blood, especially in the east. Linguistically, most of the region is not really Highland at all. This is rather disconcerting. In Aberdeenshire, Banff and Moray the speech is Northern Scots, and its use extends well up the valleys of all main rivers: Tay, Dee, Don, Deveron, Spey and Findhorn. This term 'Northern Scots' is not a loose one, but is given to a specific variety of Lowland Scots, which like English itself is a dialect of Germanic origin, distinct from the Gaelic speech which belongs to an entirely different family. This means that to-day in the region the main areas of habitation actually speak a Lowland tongue. Even Tomintoul, highest village in the Highlands, uses the Lowland dialect known as Mid-Northern Scots! Only two or three generations ago Gaelic was still spoken by many in Central Scotland. Rapid domination by Lowland speech is partly due to the fact that nearly all important towns are on or near the coast, and there Scots has been spoken since early times; but another reason which has been claimed is the readiness with which the Celt picks up foreign tongues, so that wherever there is a frontier between Celt and Saxon it is usually Celt and not Saxon who becomes bi-lingual. The increasing settlement by English incomers in recent years must further modify speech, because those people are no longer mainly confined to the large estates but are met with behind shop-counters and among the staffs of hotels and restaurants and bars or as the retired new owners of small houses in a village.

1,500 years ago, of course, the entire region was Celtic. Even then its inhabitants were not the same as those of the western seaboard. In the chapters which follow, from time to time we will come across wonderful carved stone monuments which, although many bear crosses, differ greatly from the high crosses and other monuments found in the west and in Ireland. They are the work of the Picts, the Painted Men, and whatever the Picts may have been racially they had a liberal share of the Celt's gift for imagery and decorative symbolism. The east coast was vulnerable to raiders from beyond the North Sea, and immigrants from the south also were drawn to it, so that the Celt of the Central Highlands either fused with the intruders or was driven west by them. In the coastal strip from the Tay round to Inverness the intruders became dominant. It is a fertile, populous strip, and in most parts of it there is not much trace of the Highlander in the people. They are industrious, tough, rugged, not very easy to get to know, but staunch and warm-hearted. A long tradition of fishing lingers in the coastal towns, but the photographs which show their harbours crammed with smacks and with the vessels which took the barrelled herring direct to Russian ports belong to another age. The highly-capitalised fleets from the south and from abroad have all but destroyed this once-prosperous industry, and there is something symbolic in the fact that one may look from the windows of the new Signal-Tower Museum in Arbroath and see, framed there as in a museum case, a mere handful of vessels homing into the harbour. Now even the great fish-market of Aberdeen may be threatened by that new and dubious harvest of the sea – oil. But the easterly and northerly gales of which the oil-men complain have made the people here hard-bitten and uncompromising. This has made them tough farmers too. Good land is plentiful, but the north-east has the bitterest winters of anywhere in Scotland except the high hills. Snow can lie for a long time in the fields by Ythan and Deveron. But in every sense they have built well in those parts, and there is something of the local granite in their characters. It may even help them resist the demoralisation of the big-money invasion.

In the upland portion of the Central Highlands, which in area far outweighs the rest, the population is sparse, if not quite as sparse as in the western and northern Highlands. Its main concentrations are in Strathdee, Strathdon and Strathspey, and in central Perthshire. Agriculture is important, more especially in Perthshire and Strathspey, and the alluvial valley floors are fertile and are used both for cattle-raising and for crops, barley in lower Speyside being important for supplying the distilleries. The crofts on higher ground tend to be small farms rather than the true crofts of the west. Higher again are the hill-grazings, and the Blackface and Cheviot herds which two centuries ago were as hated symbols as the redcoats have long been part of the landscape. The high hills are also, of course, grazed by the red deer, and attempts are now being made to farm this animal. This seems to be largely a response to Continental demands for venison, but in an overpopulated, over-industralised country like Britain even this small contribution towards self-maintenance should be fostered for home supply, not for export. I would go further and say for local supply, since it is time the Highlands did something to concentrate on local delicacies instead of utilising the deep-freeze to stock up imported fare in the hotels. Much of the land unusable for agriculture has come under afforestation, either carried out by the Forestry Commission or by private landowners, although new taxes seem to have been devised to foil the latter when of course they should have had every encouragement. The soft woods are destined mainly for the pulp mill at Fort William. Forestry does not, unfortunately, employ large numbers of men and therefore contributes little to stem the depopulation which is still going on. The main single industry in the Central Highlands is tourism. It has been of increasing importance ever since Victoria popularised Deeside. Its first phase launched the big sporting estates, which still have a part although much of the shooting is now syndicated or run on the lines of commercial business. For a century resorts small and not so small catered for middle class summer visitors, providing golf and fishing and hill-walking. Now tourism is big business. Many see it as the main prop of the Highlands in the future. The question is whether it will benefit the Highlander, how much of the profit will come to him and how much to incoming entrepreneurs. The sort of money needed for massive promotion has to be sought in the cities, and the profits are likely to go back there, and the sort of tourist who responds to such promotion expects a familiar pattern of diversion to which the Highland environment may well be no more than a novelty background, an alternative to a fortnight on the Costa Brava or Majorca. The Central Highlands are still full of delights for the discriminating visitor with time to linger, and it is for him

15

the succeeding chapters are written; but for him organised tourism will make things more difficult, certainly not easier.

No feature of the Highland way of life has been more shockingly abused in he name of touristic promotion than the tartan, so this may be a suitable point at which to say something about it. The romantic idea that the Highlands in ancient times were populated by clans which were instantly recognisable by their tartans is nonsense. It is a notion current for long enough, for it probably dates back to the early nineteenth century when the brothers Sobieski Stuart published *Vestiarum Scoticum,* purporting to be a collection of early records of clan tartans not for the Highlands only but also for the Lowlands. Sir Walter Scott at once attacked it as a fraud. It was however popular with tartan manufacturers, who have upheld the theory of specific clan tartans ever since. In fact, the ancient garb of the Gael was a saffron-coloured shirt, the *leine chroich,* later the great belted plaid or *feileadh-mor.* The *breacan* or tartan was in use by the seventeenth century, but there is no evidence that the pattern, the *sett,* was devised according to particular clans. The old bards would certainly have made the most of such a livery in their heroic poetry, but there is not a single reference to such a thing. Nor do early travellers like Martin record it. It is the bonnet-badge, the *suaicheantas,* a sprig of some flower or plant, which is the emblem of family. Even at the end of the eighteenth century, when the cult of Highland dress was catching on after the repeal of the Disarming Acts, tartans seem to have been selected as one might select patterns in a tailor's shop to-day, for their personal appeal, possibly influenced by fashion. Probably there was a tendency before 1745 for the immediate followers of a chief to conform to a pattern of tartan, more or less, but not because it was recognised as the family *sett.* To my mind it is likely that over the generations certain patterns tended to be associated with certain districts, determined in part by the distribution of plants used in dyeing the wool. Thus the blues and purples got from the blaeberry might be commoner in Speyside or Deeside, while tidal rock plants such as crotal belonged in coastal districts. It has to be confessed that the whole system of clan *setts* so strictly laid down to-day not only post-dates Culloden and the repressions which

1. above *Pair of Doune pistols.* 2. below *Pistol materials*

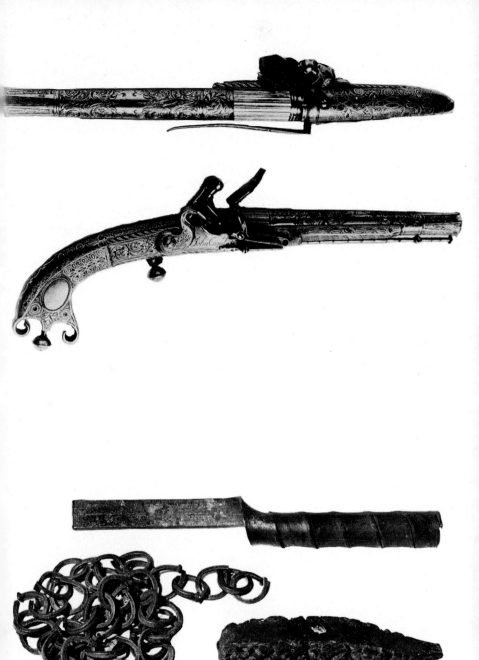

followed that battle, but may well be contemporary with the decision to issue specific tartans as part of the uniform of the newly-formed Highland regiments into which the suppressed martial ardour of the clans was diverted. The first of these was actually raised before the 'Forty-five: the Black Watch, formed in 1739, and they and only they were permitted to wear Highland garb after the rising. Other regiments followed down to the end of the century, and the use of specific tartans became a jealously-defended privilege, despite Government attempts to stop the practice. By the middle of the nineteenth century the tartan as a sign of identity was accepted not merely throughout the Highlands, where the Queen had encouraged it with enthusiasm, but throughout Scotland, which claimed as its national costume a garb which law-abiding Lowlanders once had feared and abominated!

History of course is a theme which runs through all the chapters of this book, but a thumb-nail sketch of its phases in the region as a whole should perhaps have a place here. It is convenient to begin with the Romans. In A.D.81 Agricola led an army to the Forth-Clyde line, where he set up a chain of forts; and then, provoked by Pictish threats, he probed further north by way of Perthshire and Strathmore until he brought the Pictish leader, Calgacus, to battle at Mons Graupius, which by an error in spelling has give us the name Grampian. The site of the battle used to be located somewhere in Strathmore, which certainly was on Agricola's route, but there has been a tendency to push it further north, and the late Dr Douglas Simpson even raised the possibility it might have been somewhere near the field of Culloden itself. We know Agricola subsequently sent a fleet round the north of Scotland, so that the legions could have been supported from the sea, but evidence of Roman occupation grows thinner as we go up into Aberdeenshire and wheel left to the Moray Firth. Much later Severus again led the eagles into the north. But we should be careful not to accept uncritically the familiar picture of Romans thrusting into a Highland wilderness tenanted by painted savages, for Pictland – the richer provinces of Strathmore, Angus, Aberdeenshire and Moray, at least – seems to have been inhabited by a confederation of proud tribes bred not only in the arts of war

3. above Rob Roy's gravestone. 4. below the Dunfallandy Slab, near Pitlochry

but also in the sophisticated tradition of Late Celtic culture, which had its roots all over western Europe. At the same time the Picts were by no means unfamiliar with the ways of the great Imperial province to the south of them. There are indications they may have used Roman coinage, and it is not unlikely their leading men spoke Latin at least as well as British statesmen do French or German. The Picts have left no written records for historians, but that does not mean they were inarticulate for, as Simpson has said, the uniformity of their symbols and their widespread system of ideographic art is an astonishing manifestation of their genius.

All the Central Highlands were occupied by the Picts at the time when Rome collapsed; but the edicts of the Emperors had never counted for much north of the Antonine Wall, and Rome's first lasting impact on this region came with the Christian mission of St Ninian about the beginning of the fifth century. Ninian got as far as the Orkneys. How many converts he made we do not know. A century and a half later came the Irish mission of Columba, motivated partially by the need to counter the Picts' attempts to drive out the Scots, Columba's kinsmen, from their foothold in Dalriada. Bangor, that rich training-ground of missionaries praised by St Bernard, sent St Moluag as far as eastern Pictland. At last in 844 the war between Picts and Scots ended when Kenneth MacAlpine, a Scotic king with Pictish royal blood on his mother's side, became the first king of the two peoples. At the same time the spiritual centre of Scotland was transferred from Iona to Dunkeld, deep in the Central Highlands, by the translation there of Columba's relics. Spiritually and politically this was a great era in Highland history, with the Lowlands a mere buffer state against pagan Northumbria.

From the eighth to the twelfth centuries paganism battered at the frontiers. There were unceasing Viking assaults, but their forays only occasionally penetrated the great central area. The Celtic kingdom progressed, and under Malcolm MacKenneth (1005–1034) even evolved a code of law, including a law of succession which still is the basis of Scottish practice. Macbeth, however, an able ruler naturally frowned upon by the Church because he came to power by slaying Duncan, was the last king to rule Scotland from the Highlands. He was slain and succeeded (1057) by Malcolm Canmore. Canmore moved his capital to Dunfermline and the political importance of the Highland region receded, while the Celtic element retreated before Saxon and Norman dominance. Malcolm's queen, Margaret, conceived a special enmity towards the Celtic Church. This in itself was a tragedy for the Highlands, because that Church was suited to the social system of the region, its hereditary abbots closely bound up with the clans; but by 1300 it survived only in the dwindling sect of the Culdees, whose benefices the Roman Church systematically filled with her own priests.

The Highlands nevertheless played an important part in Scotland's war for independence. From the close of the thirteenth century this restless region saw developments in the clan system, and the clan-family concept of feudalism strengthened the Crown. The King of Scots might be located far to the south but he was still *Ard-Rhigh Albann* and the father of his great family. When David II made a progress in the north among his chieftains there was the happiest relationship, and David bequeathed this to his nephew Robert II, first of that Stewart line which was to lean on Highland loyalty for nearly 400 years. At first sight, politically and socially the Highlands of the middle ages seem as tattered and fragmentary as their outline on the map, and even the central region suffered from perpetual feuds between the clans; but here again the conventional picture of the Highlands as in need of 'civilising' influence is misleading unless put into perspective with what was going on in the rest of Europe. Hume Brown long ago pointed out that Scotland had no internecine fighting on the scale of the Wars of the Roses in England or of the Burgundians and Armagnacs in France. One must not make extravagant claims for people who in certain respects must at the time have seemed to live like savages and whose hands at small provocation went to their swords, yet the burning loyalties of the clan system developed certain codes and consistencies which those other countries lacked, and its jealous regard for family tenures may have developed a pattern of rights, through which individual freedom could find expression, not to be found in societies threatened by predatory barons whom the king himself often was powerless to stop.

But with the Reformation hostility increased again between Highlands and Lowlands. Even before 1560 the Church had groped with greedy hands for clan lands, but the Reformed Kirk had nothing whatever in common with the Highlanders, their colourful feudalism and their elusive Celtic approach to life being the antithesis of the soberly regulated system of the presbyteries. And the King himself, loyally as he was regarded by the Highlanders, now found he had to curb their waywardness. Royal burghs were established in the heart of clan country, landholders were required to show their titles (1598) – documents which few of them possessed, as the Government well knew. Most attempts to weaken the clan system were resisted and defeated until the Union of the Crowns in 1603, when Lowlanders and English combined to bring 'enlightenment' to the north. An act of 1608 tried to dislocate the clan way of life by prohibiting certain weapons, and also boats. Further measures were imposed the following year, part religious, part economic, and a clause forbidding the sale of alcohol suggests the attempts to ban the sale of 'fire-water' to Red Indians. Whatever successes the new laws had, the one material thing they failed to extract from their victims was their weapons, and for another century and more the Highlander contrived to keep a sharp edge on his steel. Feuds continued to absorb some of his energies down to 1688, when Macdonell of Keppoch revenged himself on the Mackintoshes over a land dispute. But the Stewart kings found uses for the Highland Host's loyalty to the *Ard-Rhigh*. Clansmen were brought in, under Claverhouse, against the Covenanters, and in 1688 against William of Orange. Only after they formally received King James's sanction did they eventually take the oath of allegiance to William, such were their old-fashioned feudal ideas of honour. The Government's notion of honour was different, as we know from the massacre in Glencoe of the Macdonalds by troops which had accepted their hospitality the night before. The Highlands were now quite disillusioned by the behaviour of a Crown which could have made them staunchly loyal. So when in 1715 the Stewarts appealed to that loyalty they got a considerable response and their standard was raised on the Braes. But Mar was no leader. The cause failed, and failure was followed by repressive measures, among them the construction by General Wade of those roads and bridges so often met with in later pages. The Stewart standard was raised for the last time in 1745 in Glenfinnan. When the appeal went out to 'our faithful Highlanders, a people trained up and inured to arms', Charles Edward's progress through the glens was perfectly conceived to please the Celt's love of pageantry and chivalry. It is estimated that out of well over 20,000 clan warriors only about 8,000 sided with the Government, and it is no wonder that within a short time the Highland army put all Scotland in the Prince's hands and saw him hold court at Holyroodhouse. The same army might well have installed him at St James's, had it been more wisely and shrewdly led; but in December began the long withdrawal which ended on 16 April at Culloden Muir.

The revenge taken by the Government on the Highlands is no doubt a measure of how it had been terrorised by the Highlanders. Massacres beside which Glencoe is nothing took place in the glens. None claimed the price of £30,000 set on the head of fugitive Charles Edward, although one should perhaps pause to think of what the fate of such a claimant would have been. Disarming acts proscribed the possession of weapons, this time more effectively, also the Highland dress, and even bagpipes counted as a weapon of war. The Crown claimed huge areas of the country. Exile was the fate of such rebels as escaped butchery or the gallows, at least if they were prominent men, but for the rest of the people began a long tale of emigration. Some of this may have been inevitable: between the 'Forty-five and the end of the Napoleonic wars the population had almost doubled, this in a land where the means of subsistence were almost impossible to expand. The martial spirit was drawn off by the newly-created Highland regiments of the British Army, a safety-valve device for which Lord President Forbes, himself a Highlander and a man of high integrity, can claim much of the credit. The next chapter, however is perhaps as discreditable to the Government as the massacres of 1746. Many of the chiefs were beguiled into moving south to Edinburgh and London, becoming absentee landlords with much pride but without means to maintain themselves in city society in due style. Great tracts of the hills were turned into sheep-runs and rented to Lowland farmers backed by city financiers, whose rents went to the chiefs, and the miserable remnants of many a clan were driven off with extreme cruelty by the agents in those Clearances, although it should be said here that the Central Highlands suffered much less than the west and north. The broad picture of the break-up of clan society is true of all parts. Dr Johnson, that shrewd traveller and better friend of Scotland than he is sometimes given credit for being, remarked with regret on this break-up, and particularly deplored the educating of chieftains' sons in the south of England where, he said, 'they will be tamed into insignificance'.

Upon this desolate scene presently dawned the Victorian age. It was to perpetuate the economy of the deer forest and establish the tradition of the grouse moor, and to scatter mock baronial buildings in glen and strath; but in the Central Highlands in particular it brought back at least a curious imitation of the clan-family pattern of living, false in many of its values, yet with a queer thread of wisdom running through it, which is more than can be said of any measure which had emanated from the Mother of Parliaments applying to the Highlands. It is not for nothing that the old Queen's memory is kept extraordinarily fresh on Deeside even to-day. It may have started with nothing more than sentiment, but the Highlanders did respond to the idea of a feudal matriarchy which she set up at Balmoral. Her passion for trappings such as tartan and her revival of the gatherings were balm to a people whose feelings had been trampled upon for generations, scorn and amusement though such things have produced in many critics. As far as the Balmoral estates are concerned, the Queen, no doubt unintentionally, created a latter-day equivalent of the old clan relationships and both she and her people there were made happy by the experience. In her lengthier and lengthier residences on Deeside she came to know hundreds of folk and interested herself in their affairs, helped them, worshipped with them – more earnestly than His Grace of Canterbury at the time approved! – and came nearer than any sovereign for centuries had done to deserving the title of *Ard-Rhigh Albann*. The things she did were simple and personal, in no way remedying political and economic wrongs done over the centuries, but in a strange way they went to the heart of the Highland problem and are not without a lesson for to-day. That problem now looms larger than ever. There are some who do deeply understand what underlies it, but new forms of exploitation or of misrule are showing themselves against which the clansman may have need of a weapon both subtler and stronger than the broadsword which his forebears hid among the thatch.

The future of the Highlands holds many interesting problems, some of which are being decided before all concerned have had adequate time to think about them. The Central Highlands in themselves are a large area relative to the United Kingdom, but the inhabitants are few and so, as a mere particle in a democracy, they have all too little say in their future. They tend to be ground between the upper and the nether millstones of two powerful forces which can be labelled as Conservation and Exploitation. These are perhaps rather emotive terms. The conservationists are not necessarily or in all circumstances dedicated to the best interests of the Highlanders, nor are all exploiters bent on overriding those interests; but both sides tend to be looking at the Highlands from the outside.

To take the conservationists first: they are not made up entirely of reactionary lairds trying to keep things as they are. Indeed there are probably far more reactionaries in Lowland cities and south of the Border, even in the stockbroker belt. The rat-race of a tottering urban civilisation has turned the eyes of many of its victims towards what seems to them to be the last refuge of sanity in these islands, a land where they may breathe pure air and sip unpolluted burns and escape the clamour of cars and aeroplanes and that invention of the devil, the portable transistor radio. Already there is a vast influx of 'white settlers' to the remoter glens. Some, who come to integrate with the community and live their lives there, are welcome. They may eventually become Highlanders. Others – and unhappily they are far more numerous – who buy up property for the occasional holiday visit or dump caravans for the same purpose, bringing food-hall supplies with them from their city-suburbs, do nothing for the Highlands and only succeed in inflating the market-value of properties far beyond the means of the local people. And then there is the public park attitude, aiming to preserve the Highlands for those hundreds of thousands in the Lowlands and the south who look upon the Highlands as a glorified green belt brought within easy reach by the internal combustion engine, a place in which they have no interest except as a pleasant background for the familiar ploys and games which they bring with them. Where in former times summer visitors delighted in what the country had to offer, the trout-streams, the hill-walks, the resinous-scented woods, the hum of bees among the heather, the newcomers demand facilities for organised sport, car and caravan parks, access roads, and at some points cinemas, swimming pools, bingo halls, to say nothing of public lavatories at strategic beauty spots. To classify those people under the conservationists may seem a lame sort of satire, but to rope off large areas of a countryside for such purposes is in fact conservation, of the wrong sort, because it fails to recognise the right of the inhabitants to manage things in their own best interest.

Positive conservation is quite another matter. It involves close study of the place and people, and evaluation of their real interests, determining of a balance between the maintenance of a heritage and the introduction of growth-points which will generate natural progress. Several bodies are involved in this, such as the Nature Conservancy and the National Trust for Scotland, the Forestry and the Countryside Commissions, and one must not forget the commercial organisations such as the North of Scotland Hydro-Electric Board which, in supplying the Highlands with power, have gone to considerable lengths to preserve amenities and to avoid interference with, for example, the salmon runs. There is no lack of protagonists for the *status quo* and indeed for restoring the *status quo ante* the damage done by centuries of exploitation, ranging from biologists and ecologists to historians and antiquaries, and fortunately many of these are well aware that true conservation of an environment and heritage requires the presence of a healthy, happy population, with ample opportunities and confidence in the future. The Highlands have to be more than a good place to visit: they have to be a viable proposition for those who live there.

So we turn to the exploiters, or perhaps we should call them developers. By many placed high on the list of suitable 'industries' is tourism. Large-scale tourism involves a proliferation of facilities from modern hotels to ski schools, wild-life parks and the rest. But I have already touched on this and briefly given my views, and will not revert to it. More interesting from the point of view of making the Highlands viable as a place to live in is the development of natural resources and native skills. Agriculture, like tourism, has already been mentioned, likewise forestry; but neither can do a great deal to help keep the younger generation from leaving the area for more lucrative jobs elsewhere. One natural resource which has been exploited with considerable success since the war is water-power, and a large proportion of the available head of water has been harnessed by damming glens, tunnelling mountains and building power-stations, with little injury to amenity, as I have said earlier; and this enterprise has made electricity available even to remote dwellings, with a surplus to 'export' to the national grid. This has been a real contribution to an easier life, and it also makes possible the introduction of industries hitherto unthought of. If I have any reservation on this it would be on the cultural effect of dragging the Highlands within reach of the radio and TV networks, ultimately stamping them with the same pattern of outlook as the rest of the country. But from the economic aspect it must always be kept in mind that the immense power potential possessed by Switzerland and Norway just does not exist in the Highlands, for the scale of mountains is so much less and there are no permanent snow-fields to feed the rivers, and in the Central Highlands in particular rainfall is much less than in the west, which takes the brunt of the Atlantic weather. Industry based on natural resources then, the land apart, is not very extensive. The tweed industries of the Borders and the Western Isles – although the latter, unhappily, is threatened – has no counterpart in the Central Highlands. There are, of course, the distilleries whose characteristic outlines may be recognised in many a glen, and about which something will be found in the chapter on the Lower Spey, but here again whisky-making does not employ large numbers.

The Highlands and Islands Board's policy of 'growth-centres' has had a little success, most noticeably around Inverness; but the attraction of outside firms, even if accompanied by attempts to persuade emigrant Highlanders to return to their homeland, seems to raise some of the problems involved in heart-transplant operations, including the possibility of ultimate rejection in the sense that the new venture may never really become integrated with the community. If one sinks enough money in a project one can probably establish an alien industry almost anywhere and keep it going for a time, but there seems to be a better chance of success in seeking for existing growth-points, however modest, and doing all that is possible to foster them, even if the result is never spectacular in terms of the economist's book. A way of life may be more important than a big profit-margin, especially in inflationary times when profits are quite unreal anyway. The Central Highland area seems better suited to small-scale craft industries based on individual skills rather than highly-mechanised industries depending on transport and imported raw materials. I do not mean by this that the straths should be peppered with art-craft studios turning out souvenirs for the tourists or little 'creations' from river-pebbles or driftwood. What I am thinking of is the development of industrial hand-skills using materials for the most part available or produced locally. Textiles for discriminating buyers obviously are among these: the Elgin mills under the late E. S. Harrison showed the way in this field long ago, although they did make some use of rarer imported fleeces such as Cashmere and Vicuna. Timber offers at least as many opportunites. New planting could be put to better uses than the production of newsprint. The Scandinavian nations have made their timber, and their textiles, contribute substantially to their amenities and way of life, and the inroads of unsightly brick and concrete structures which have spoiled so many towns and villages in the Central Highlands could have been avoided by reliance on local materials.

Communications have always been a special problem in this area. In anywhere so sparsely populated every new mile of road is a heavy burden on the ratepayers, and subsidies from central funds are not usually expended primarily to benefit local interests, whether in the time of General Wade or now. There is a big problem of trunk-road building under way to facilitate long-distance haulage, stimulated especially by the needs of North Sea oil developments, whether at Aberdeen and neighbouring towns or points beyond Inverness such as Nigg. The vast expenditure on those schemes, notably on the Great North Road, could have been slashed if existing rail facilities had been improved. It is the railways, not the road-systems, which are the real lifelines of the Highland communities, because even the best-engineered roads cannot always be kept open during severe winters. Nor has the emphasis on roads done anything to compensate locals by bringing improved public transport, and the private car has therefore become essential in many areas, so that when increased taxes on petrol are not compensated for in any way for the Highlands it is hardly surprising if Highlanders suspect this is just further evidence that the attitude of authority towards them has not greatly changed since the seventeenth century.

As to education, in the central region as a whole the situation is very different from that in the northern and western Highlands, where it is usual rather than exceptional for pupils of secondary schools either to be transported long distances daily, or boarded out. This does of course happen also in the Central Highlands, but in the more populous areas educational facilities compare well with those anywhere else in the kingdom, and some of the schools are famous. As there are no Gaelic-speaking localities, the vexed question of Gaelic in schools does not arise. It is when we come to further education that the able or ambitious student may have to look outside the Highlands to get what he wants. Aberdeen does come within the region as I have defined it, and it has always been the nearest thing to the Highlanders' university, but it is very much on the periphery, and the siting of a new university at Stirling, within thirty miles of both Edinburgh and Glasgow, against the claims of a Highland town, was a quite incomprehensible decision. The obvious site was Inverness. It could have become in a short time a major centre for Celtic studies, and also for the special problems of the Highland area, social, economic, agricultural. The argument that it was too remote to attract teachers of high status verges on the frivolous. It would have offered that kind of *raison d'être* and specific challenge which is so sadly lacking in most of the newly-created universities, and would have provided a platform for critical minds to thrash out the controversial issues facing the Highlands and to voice their needs in tones of authority.

Vast tracts of the Central Highlands for two centuries have been in the hands of private landowners, successors to the clans which were broken in 1746. Now it is the turn of the private estates to come under threat, for both economic and political reasons. The land, it is claimed, belongs to the people ... 'The people' is a convenient abstraction. In point of fact it means no one. Ownership of land must be real. The land needs to be loved, a friend of mine said many years ago in one of his books. He is not a sentimentalist, the man who wrote that. He has long experience of land management, and his advice is much sought after in high places. What it adds up to is that land must belong to people, not to *the* people. But which people? Certainly not the people who are prepared to impose the materialism of our doomed urban society on a region to which historically it is totally foreign. In the past the Highlands have suffered tragically by their sometimes quixotic refusal to conform, but if they can be persuaded not to lose sight of this attitude entirely it might help them to survive the World Crisis rather more easily than their neighbours! There is probably good land enough in the glens and straths to make basic subsistence possible for the few hundred thousand Highlanders.

CHAPTER ONE

Dunblane and the South-West

Dunblane may not seem to be a Highland town; but a Roman or a redcoat, or indeed a tourist, trying to penetrate the wall of peaks which notch the northern horizon, must stop here to take stock and decide which way to go. He can go north-east up the Allan Water to Strathearn, or west to the Trossachs, Balquhidder and beyond. Dunblane is in fact one of the two main Highland gateway towns, the other being Perth. Like Perth, it draws a good deal of its importance and interest from this fact.

It is a cathedral town, and well worth spending some time in before looking further. In origin it is very much one with the Highland way of life. Dun-Blane means the Hill of Blane – St Blaan was a missionary Irish monk of the sixth century who came from Bangor in Ireland and founded churches from Cumberland to Aberdeenshire. Nothing remains of any link with the old Celtic Church here now, except perhaps the ancient stone cross found under the nave, preserved at the west end of the north aisle. It is one of many stones found along the length of the Highland boundary wherever the early missions penetrated or settled. Such stones are reminders that the Highlands of old were not a wild wilderness beyond the fringe of civilisation but part of that refuge of Christianity from which the missionaries again went out into pagan Europe to revive the faith. Our outlook is so founded on Roman writers such as Tacitus who looked upon places like the Highlands as beyond the pale that we still think that to go north is to go among strangers. We should pay more attention to those ancient stones, uninscribed and therefore unvocal though most of them are, as evidence of a faith and a culture largely forgotten, and this is why

31

attention will be drawn to them in dark corners and over-grown churchyards again and again in this book. Here and in other places along the Highland border the Celtic Church survived in communities which became the sects of the Culdees. Their college at Dunblane had to survive fire and plunder by both Briton and Dane.

Dunblane is a small town of narrow streets with an old-world air. Its people take pride in it, but especially they take pride in the Cathedral Church of St Blane, and a great deal has been done to preserve and restore the fabric and the nearer precincts. It was David I, that 'sair sanct for the croun', who elevated Dunblane into a bishopric about 1150, and the first cathedral came into being during the half-century that followed, but the only part of this which has survived is the lower portion of the tower. There was not enough money for its upkeep, and one Friar Clement had to make a journey to Rome to secure the means to restore the roof. During the centuries which followed the cathedral suffered further heavy damage. Edward I ripped the lead from the roof for the siege-engines which he built to reduce Stirling Castle. In 1559 the Earl of Argyll desecrated it, though he forebore to wreck the choir. As it stands now, the lower two-thirds of the tower is Norman, topped by a sixteenth-century addition, the nave is in the first Pointed style, the choir is a little later, and the north aisle or Lady Chapel in date comes somewhere between the tower and the nave. Despite Argyll's depredations the cathedral retains some very beautiful ornament. The west door, though simple, is richly and deeply moulded, and the three windows above were singled out by Ruskin in a lecture to the Philosophical Institution of Edinburgh in words reminiscent of a passage in *The Stones of Venice*. Why, he asks, is that west window beautiful? – 'Because in its great contours it has the form of a forest leaf, and because in its decoration he has used nothing but forest leaves. He was no common man who designed that cathedral of Dunblane. I know nothing so perfect in its simplicity, and so beautiful so far as it reaches, in all the Gothic with which I am acquainted . . . Instead of putting a mere formal dog's tooth, as everybody else did at the time, he went down to the woody bank of the sweet river beneath the rocks on which he was building, and then took up a few of the fallen leaves that lay by and he set them in his arch side by side for ever.'

The cathedral possesses something else unique in Scotland in a series of richly-carved, canopied choir-stalls of the fifteenth century. They are known as the Ochiltree stalls, as nearby is an effigy of Bishop Ochiltree, who died in 1447. Only in King's College Chapel, in Aberdeen, is there anything comparable. Other features fairly uncommon in a Scots church are the recumbent stone effigies of Malise, eighth Earl of Strathearn, and his wife. In the floor of the north choir are three blue stones believed at one time to have covered the graves of Lady Margaret Drummond and her sisters. The story goes that James IV as a youth fell in love with Lady Margaret and secretly married her, and indeed had a daughter by her. When he came to the throne James prepared to make public his marriage, but a Court party had determined he should marry an English princess and, at the official wedding breakfast, Margaret and her sisters were poisoned. Broken-hearted, the king arranged a magnificent burial in the cathedral of which the uncle of the sisters, Sir Walter Drummond, was Dean.

It is the westward road out of Dunblane we shall take in this chapter. Away on the left is the broad, alluvial plain through which the River Forth winds to Stirling and the sea, a low land which indeed the sea once covered. This is Flanders Moss. Until the eighteenth century a bog laced with dark tarns, its interest for anyone on his way to the Highlands lies in the great reclamation scheme instituted by Lord Kames, which gave work to hundreds of Highlanders made destitute by repressive measures following the 'Forty-five. They drained the marshes and cut the peat, and the moss-lairds, as they were called, became the first to prosper on this magnificent farm-land. Our route, however, joins a tributary of the Forth, the Teith. This flows away through the lands of several great houses – Ochtertyre, Blair Drummond, Keir, which once belonged to Sir William Stirling-Maxwell, the historian and art critic who first introduced the splendours of Spanish painting to this country – and meets the westward road at the village of Doune.

Doune is of special account for anyone interested in Highland history, although most tourists flash through it unaware. Motorists obeying the speed-limit sign may slow down in time to see another sign at the entrance to the village, a pair of pistols crossed. This has meaning for hardly anyone to-day, but it points to the very special part which Doune played in the life of the Highlander, particularly in the eighteenth century. Here in this village were made many of the finest pistols in which the clansmen took delight, and its reputation lasted for two centuries or more. The weapons made by a few families here were perfected over the years to become such masterpieces of the gunsmith's art that they found their way as presents to the most fastidious courts in Europe. They can be seen in museums everywhere: In Dresden, in the Musée d'Artillerie in Paris, in the Metropolitan Museum of Art in New York, in the Tower of London. There is a superb gold-mounted pair in Windsor Castle, and twin Scottish pistols have a place among the relics of King Gustavus Adolphus in the Royal Armoury in Stockholm.

If I linger around this small village and its products, it is not because any of the pistols can now be seen here – the nearest examples are probably several in the Smith Institute in Stirling, ten miles back – but because those pistols symbolise a very important aspect of Highland history: Celtic pride and love of putting on a brave show. Doune must have been rather like some of those frontier towns in the western states of America to which Indian braves would come in search of pretty weapons which were often turned against the frontiersmen themselves. The names of the great Doune pistol-smiths, Campbell and Caddell, Murdoch and Christie, are not all of them Highland. The chief characteristic of the Doune pistol is that is it all metal: butt, stock and barrel; but its lines flow as delicately as if it were carved in soft wood, and its engraved decoration sometimes is nearly as intricate as lace. Typically, the butt ends in a scroll or 'ram's horn'. There is no trigger-guard. Trigger and the pricker lodged between the horns of the butt have silver finials and in the best pistols silver inlay is beaten into the surface decoration. In the rarest pieces of all gold takes the place of silver, but the only two such pairs I have seen or heard of are the Campbell pistols at Windsor and a similar brace stolen many years ago from the Colville Collection in Edinburgh Castle, now almost certainly in the United States. It may seem

5. above *Grandtully Castle.* *6.* below *Edinample house, Loch Earn*

strange that the basic metal from which the pistols were made came from old horseshoe-nails, which were twisted into a crude chain and then hammered into a thick ribbon that was finally coiled and beaten around a metal rod of approximately the right bore.

The Disarming Acts which followed Prince Charles Edward's rebellion of the 'Forty-five did not terminate the Doune pistol-trade. This is surprising. All clansmen were forbidden to carry weapons, to wear the kilt or the tartan, or even to play the bagpipes. Doune must have found customers in the Lowlands as the trade went on until the end of the eighteenth century; but the first *Statistical Account of Scotland,* compiled just before 1800, laments that when John Murdoch retires from business this traditional industry will be dead. In the end it received the compliment of having two sorts of imitator: the sophisticated makers of magnificent gilded and enamelled costume pieces of 'Highland' appearance such as the Clanranald pistols in the National Museum of Antiquities or those painted by Sir Henry Raeburn in his portrait of Macdonnell of Glengarry, or the commercial imitators who supplied Highland regiments in the early days, notably one Bissell, a Birmingham gunsmith!

Doune is a quiet, pleasant village, secluded from passing traffic. It lies where the Teith is joined by the Ardoch burn, and this junction is the site of one of the most impressive medieval castles in Scotland, described by the late Dr Douglas Simpson as 'the highest achievement of perfected castellar construction' in the country. Dominating the angle between the two waters, it has tremendous frontal strength, and its embattled mien advertises it as the stronghold of some personage of power. The man who built it was in fact the Regent of Scotland, Robert, Duke of Albany, who held the country during the English captivity of James I, and the time of its building was the last years of the fourteenth century. Robert was one of those great barons who manipulated the affairs of their country by means of private armies, but who therefore led a perpetually dangerous existence. There is evidence that he had much popular support, and certainly did not maintain himself by taxing the people, but men of this sort had to have strong places to operate from. Doune Castle combines with great military strength

7. Loch Voil

extensive accommodation for retainers, and the two needs are married in the extraordinary north-east tower, which even in its present state is 80 feet high. The low, narrow entrance at the base is, of course a concession to strength, easy to defend; but inside and above the entrance is a baronial hall 35 feet long with a big double fireplace, a chamber which, hung with arras and suitably furnished, must have had considerable grandeur. And it was to accommodate more than one prominent figure in history after Albany's day. In 1502 Doune passed in liferent to Margaret Tudor, daughter of Henry VII of England and wife of James IV of Scotland. It was a favourite residence of Mary Queen of Scots. In the 'Forty-five it had a Jacobite garrison, and committed to it were several prisoners from the field of Falkirk, among them the Rev. John Hume, the minister who scandalised the Kirk by writing for the theatre. There were escapes from it; but to storm its battlements would have been far more difficult. The keep had its own well, and the usual siege-practice of building an assault tower and wheeling it up against the battlements was here ruled out by the uneven ground below the 40-foot curtain-wall.

Doune's link with the economy of the Highlands went much further than pistol-making. Two hundred years ago the Doune Tryst was an important cattle-market, where the dealers met with the drovers bringing their beasts in from Mull and Oban in the west, from Skye and the Hebrides and other parts of the north-west. Dr A. R. B. Haldane brought together the fascinating story of the drove-roads of Scotland in a book published in 1952. A casual stranger is apt to think of the Highlands as a picturesque background to a history of tribal wars, and it is easy to overlook the patient annual rounding up of cattle from the glens and the isles and the long, long trek that ended in southern English markets. It might be thought nothing would be left but skin and bone, but Defoe relates how in Norfolk, for instance, the rich grasslands rendered the black cattle 'monstrously fat' and 'delicious for taste', in fact ready for Smithfield. The drovers probably risked as many dangers as any clansman in a foray. There would be relief among the drovers to get their beasts out of the narrow defiles and across the torrents when they came in sight of Doune, although measured in miles the journeys of many of them had a long way to go. But at Doune many of the cattle changed hands, as many as 10,000 at one Autumn Tryst.

It is after Doune that one begins to sense the change from the Lowlands to the Highlands. Those great pillars of the entrance way, on the left Ben Ledi, the Hill of God, and on the right Ben Vorlich and its outlier, Stuc a Chroin, have been visible for long enough – they can be recognised from some top-storey flats in Edinburgh fifty miles away! – but now they loom large, and can be seen as flankers of a narrow pass leading ultimately to the western Highlands. Before it lies the small town of Callander, its main street in summer at most hours choked with buses and tourists, many of them here because of the town's fictional alternative name of Tannochbrae; but it has always been a popular resort, because at this point the road divides and one may either go north into the Central Highands proper or west into that area of mini-Highlands loosely embraced by the name of the Trossachs.

About the derivation of this name there is still much uncertainty. A writer as scholarly as Douglas Simpson accepts the Gaelic *na Troiseachan*, a plural meaning 'the cross-places'. Other commentators, including the *Encyclopaedia Britannica,* have dismissed this in favour of the Rev. Patrick Graham's derivation of 'rough or bristled territory', which is considered more fitting to the scenery; but I have doubts if one of those terms is more fitting than the other, and translations of what is apparently obsolete Gaelic are wide open to speculation. You could call the Trossachs a 'cross-place', between two lochs; with their hummocky hills, bosky with birches and spikey with pines, they can well be called 'bristled'. And what is, or what are, the Trossachs anyway? According to the map the name applies to a very small area, almost a point, at the eastern end of Loch Katrine, although there is no actual village so called, but in common usage it can be extended to cover all Loch Katrine and Loch Achray, and anything between the peaks of Ben Venue and Ben A'an. The map, in fact, reads here like a marriage of fact and romantic fiction, representing Ellen's Isle and the Goblin's Cave as every bit as real as the A 821. One might indeed label this a Poets' Reserve. Whereas in other Highland areas the guidemarks range from stone circles to castles, here one takes one's bearings from couplets and quatrains and at some points has to stop and hear out an entire canto. Quite how the poets discovered the Trossachs in the first place remains something of a mystery. Sir Walter Scott certainly was familiar with the area before the eighteenth century ended. William and Dorothy Wordsworth were there almost as early, and they came because 'the Trosachs' already had some sort of romantic reputation in England. James Hogg, the Ettrick Shepherd, was there too in 1803, reporting to Scott. Southey wrote lyrically about it all. And the author of that multi-volume work, *The Beauties of Scotland*, Robert Forsyth, in 1806 penned as romantic a description as anyone:

> When the Traveller enters the Trosachs, there is such an assemblage of wildness and rude grandeur as beggars all description, and fills the mind with the most sublime conceptions. It seems as if a whole mountain had been torn in pieces, and frittered down by a convulsion of the earth, and the huge fragments of rocks and hills scattered in confusion for two miles from the east end, and by the sides of Loch Catherine. The access to the lake is through a narrow pass of half a mile in length, such as Aeneas had in his dreary passage to visit his father's home, *vastoque immanis hiatu*.

It is sometimes thought the Trossachs were singled out merely because they are the most accessible part of the Highlands, a day's coach-ride from Glasgow even two centuries ago. There may be some substance in this, but it should be remembered that the taste of those times was repelled by the uncompromising grandeur of such scenery as the precipices of Buchaille Etive Mor or An Teallach, which appeal to the realist and rock-climbing tastes of. to-day, and I seem to recall that Ruskin thought even the Trossachs' peaks a little too high for beauty! The romantics preferred their scenery to be more nearly on the scale of a gentleman's property, with everything neatly in place, the savagery on the whole to be at the discretion of their own imaginations. But it should also be remembered that the Trossachs of those times were in fact a little more truly of the 'untamed' north than they are now, and that

Wordsworth's Highland beauty chattered to her sisters not in English but in 'Irish'.

To get full enjoyment out of the Trossachs, then, it is fully proper to accept *The Lady of the Lake* in particular, and some of its contemporary literature in general, as the best guidebooks. This is not another gentle laugh at a tourist mecca. I am simply indicating that one should go there in the right mood, as one does with the opera, and for once set aside the commentaries of people who reduce their mountains to a catalogue of pitches and traverses. Let every Allt-na-this or that become Monan's rill. One certainly does not want to urge that visitors go hill-walking again in high-heeled shoes equipped with nothing more practical than a book of verse, with our mountain-rescue teams so overworked, but it is rather nice to have a reserve where the hill-paths are not all tenanted by chains of dedicated young experts hung about with nylon ropes and ironmongery. I still have a sneaking preference for meeting with tweeds rather than scarlet wind-cheaters among the high hills . . .

As for guide-books, more than once it has been remarked how accurately Scott painted his landscapes, down to details of flora and fauna, despite the extravagance of his language. By contrast, another literary achievement which I have never seen recommended as companion for a visit to the Trossachs is that one-time classic, Miss Jane Porter's *The Scottish Chiefs*. There used to be a copy of this extraordinary book in every household – mine has my grandfather's name in it, with the date 1856 – and it was first published in 1810, which is the year of *The Lady of the Lake*. It was translated into half-a-dozen languages, and for some reason got itself banned by Napoleon. It tells the story of Sir William Wallace in the form of a romance, and if one wants to see the Trossachs through the spectacles of the truly 'Gothick' vision of the time this in its earlier pages is the book to do it with. Of 'Glenfinlass', for example:

> The awful entrance to this sublime valley, struck the whole party with a feeling that made them pause. It seemed as if to those sacred solitudes, hidden in the very bosom of Scotland, no hostile foot dared to intrude. Murray looked at Ker: 'We go, my friend, to arouse the genius of our country!'

Both Scott and Miss Porter saw the Trossachs as a sort of impenetrable fastness. Both saw the place as the refuge of some indomitable, chivalrous spirit, Scott putting his innermost citadel upon Ellen's Isle in Loch Katrine, Miss Porter placing hers in Glenfinglas. If Scott's topography is the more reliable, we have to remember Miss Porter was writing far away in Thames Ditton; but to set the scene and the mood, those two authors are essential, for the Trossachs must be looked on as a period piece.

Queen Victoria took *The Lady of the Lake* with her, of course, in her visit of September 1869, fully recorded in the second volume of her Highland journal. As always, she makes interesting comments: for example, that all the 'picturesque lasses and children' here speak the Gaelic, so that the Trossachs only a century ago still remained culturally inviolate despite the fact that the Queen records: 'We met (as we had done from the first) several large coaches, but with only outside seats, full of tourists.' There was a steamer on Loch Katrine too – 'the very same we had been on under such different circumstances in 1859 on the 14th of October in dreadful weather, thick mist and heavy rain, when my beloved Husband and I opened the *Glasgow Waterworks*.' Her memories are 'melancholy and yet sweet', as when she found on the path by the lochside 'some of the same white pebbles which my dearest Albert picked up and had made into a bracelet for me'. But in spite of such reminders she had constant delight in what she saw, both scenery and people, which 'all make beloved *Scotland* the proudest, finest country in the world.'

After a hundred years and more of tourism, one would expect to find the Trossachs of to-day some kind of caricature of the Highland scene, but this is not the case. The 'large coaches' are certainly there in plenty, with their destination boards of 'Romantic Northern Scotland' and the like, but it is my impression neither coaches nor cars are any thicker on the ground than they are in many much remoter parts of the country. Indeed, they may be less so. One brilliant August afternoon I made a spot-check of car registration numbers at a point near Brig o' Turk and found that Scottish numbers as against the rest were, roughly, as one to twenty, and it may be inferred that the average Scot visits the

Trossachs only once or twice in a lifetime. It is his loss. This is not the grandest scenery in Scotland, nor has it much in the way of impressive castles or ancient sites, but there is a kind of gentle, leisurely beauty rather more hard to find further north. It is due in part to the vegetation. There is a minimum of coniferous coverage here, by Highland standards, and to the inevitable birch are added oak and beech and other deciduous trees. In autumn this makes for a compromise between the best of lowland and highland features, for the background peaks are blue and craggy enough even if they offer no great change to the climber. And the natural beauty is helped by the fact that there are few concessions to the motorist, who has to go cautiously along a narrow, winding road, much overhung by trees and dappled by sunbeams, his attention distracted by glimpses of Loch Vennachar – conditions which county councils elsewhere have usually done their best to rationalise out of existence. The stern eye of the Glasgow Water Board may have helped too. Eventually they raised the level of Loch Katrine by, I think, 17 feet, and in so doing obliterated the Silver Strand at least as Scott saw it; but without them surely there would have been a through road to Loch Lomond with all that would have meant, instead of a ban on cars approaching the loch. As it is, there is a pleasant walk along the north shore, carved out of the rock, and in twenty minutes most of the strollers have been outdistanced, so that even at the height of the season it is possible to be completely alone on this road. As Queen Victoria recorded, the Trossachs end of the loch is more attractive than the western part. It is thickly wooded, even on the promontories and on Ellen's Isle itself, which properly is called Eilean Melach, and overhung by the romantically knobbly mass of Beinn Bhreac and Ben Venue. On the north shoulder of the last can be seen the dark gash of the Coire nan Uruisgean, otherwise the Goblin's Cave, although the meaning of the Gaelic is the corrie or gully of the wild men, or *Urisks*, who were not exactly what we think of as goblins, but more of a cross between man and goat. Higher on the shoulder is 'the wild pass of Beal-nam-Bo', otherwise the Bealach nam Bo, or Pass of the Cattle. It marks the old drove route from the west which came by way of Glen Gyle and the south shore of Loch Katrine, but had to climb high over the shoulder of the ben to avoid a precipitous barrier. James Hogg drove cattle over this route long before he reported on the Trossachs to Sir Walter Scott.

The western gateway to the central Highlands is the Pass of Leny. Ben Ledi to the left is much greater in mass than the Trossachs hills, and although there is nothing as lofty on the other side the forested slopes mask a succession of outliers which, unseen, rear higher and higher in the north to the ultimate peaks of Stuc a Chroin and Ben Vorlich. Soon the confronting slopes plunge into the waters of Loch Lubnaig, to the eastern edge of which the road clings closely all the way. As the glen opens out into Strathyre the village of the name appears. A mile or two north-westwards the cottages of Balquhidder village can be seen strung out along the base of the hills. It can be reached by turning left at Strathyre, or by doing the same thing a little further on at Kingshouse, which still looks over an area of flat, cultivated lands with the fine trees and cornfields recorded in the Queen's diary. Here again is a road which leads to no outlet, and which consequently has not impelled the road engineers to straighten its bends or flatten its hills, so that the motorist is forced to take notice of his beautiful surroundings. After a mile or two comes the straggling Kirkton of Balquhidder. The place of pilgrimage here is the kirk itself, on the high ground to the right. There is an older kirk, with yews rising from within its ruins, and before its door is the grave of Rob Roy.

It is a modest grave for one who created such a stir, a flat stone flanked by another for his wife, Helen, and a second for two sons, the three surrounded by an iron rail; but the very fact that Rob was able to die peacefully in his bed in the heart of his home country itself commemorates the blend of cunning with courage which he possessed.

The eagle, he was lord above,
And Rob was lord below.

The eagle may still lord it somewhere above the Braes of Balquhidder – there will be something to say about this presently – and the legend of Rob continues to lord it over the whole of this MacGregor country as Robin Hood's does Sherwood Forest. In making Rob into something of a Robin Hood, Scott did not romanticise entirely, but there was a great deal of the rascal in the man, and he inherited a long tale of ancestral trouble-making which brought letters of fire and sword to be issued against 'the wicked clan Gregor, so long continuing in blood, slaughter, theft and robbery', as a document of 1558 has it. Rob was of the stuff of heroes of fiction. On the one hand, he was decently educated and had a proper respect for learning; on the other, he had a splendid physique and was a masterly swordsman with a phenomenal reach which made him truly formidable in a fight. He possessed the lands of Inversnaid and Craig Royston, and set out to be respectable enough as a cattle dealer and stockman; but unhappily reavers from the north raided his herds and forced him to recruit a band of protective guards, and after a time he began to lend those guards, for a consideration, to his neighbours. Soon he was extorting dues from all and sundry, an elaborate system of blackmail which landowners in the district tried to evade at their peril. Not that his neighbours had any scruples themselves. A web of feuds and acts of vengeance was spun which had him entangled throughout most of his life. He took sides in the quarrels of the great families of the west, notably the Montroses and Argyles; but the event which got him into gravest danger was the rebellion of 1715, in which he sided with the Jacobites and was an officer in the Pretender's army at the battle of Sheriffmuir. Here the wily Rob with his clansmen remained on a hill and watched the battle, not out of cowardice, which would have been quite out of character, but because of the friendly sentiments which he felt for the general on the other side, Argyle. Edinchip, the house of the MacGregor of MacGregor to-day, just over the shoulder of Auchtoomore Hill from Balquhidder, possesses a seventeenth-century powder-horn with the inscription: LORD THOV ME DEFEND FROM SUBTIL SORT OF THOSE THAT FRIENDSHIP ME PRETEND AND ARE MY MORTAL FOES. I have sometimes wondered if Rob ever contemplated this horn. But this cunning of his stood him in good stead when the Government set a price of £1,000 on his head, for somehow he escaped both scaffold and exile. The spiritual course which he steered was subtle too. Born a Presbyterian, as a friendly gesture towards the Earl of Perth he turned to Rome, yet so lightly did he regard his adopted faith that, as Scott relates, he commented that extreme unction was 'a great waste of oil.'

Queen Victoria spent some time examining the little kirk at Balquhidder, and it is well worth while to emulate her. The Rob Roy burial stone is interesting in itself. It is rather rudely carved with a figure and a sword, and one of its companion stones actually carries the arms of the MacGregors; but although Rob is buried somewhere in the churchyard the three stones appear to have been assembled side by side as a memorial rather than as covers to the grave itself. They are much more ancient than the people they now commemorate. Sword-bearing slabs of this sort are characteristic of the western, not the Central Highlands, although these are poor examples, with none of the mastery of design to be seen at Keils in Knapdale, or on Iona or Oronsay. They might be of the fifteenth or sixteenth century, brought from the west, or again they might be rather later attempts to follow the old tradition. The ruined church itself carries the date 1631. It is on the site of an earlier church, the Eaglais Beag or Little Church, which in the sixteenth century the MacGregors desecrated by carrying to it the bloody head of the King's Forester in Glenartney, on which the clansmen were made by their Chief to swear to protect the murderers. A little higher up is the present parish church, opened just four years before the Queen described it as 'very pretty'. It contains some interesting relics. The old font, which the Queen refers to as if then it lay outside, is a roughly-fashioned bowl of stone which may well be early medieval and might have come from the monastic cell which once stood in the field beyond the road. Against the north wall is a stone slab known as the St Angus Stone, with a rudely carved figure in outline grasping in its hands something which could be a chalice. This has been dated to the eighth or ninth century, which would associate it with the Celtic church which preceded a Culdee community in the neighbourhood. but I am inclined to think it may be the grave-slab of an ecclesiastic and of about the same period as the stones which commemorate Rob Roy and his family. Close to it is the old session chest, iron-bound, now containing the bell of the ruined church, dated 1684. The chest is believed to have belonged to Black Duncan Campbell of Glenorchy, who died as early as

1631, and it does seem to be of this period. Nearby are cases containing Gaelic bibles. The minister of the ruined church between 1664 and 1685 was a Gaelic scholar of some note, the Reverend Robert Kirk, and one of these books, known as Bishop Bedell's Bible, was presented to the church in 1688 by a famous natural philosopher who gave his name to one of the best-known laws of physics, Robert Boyle. Boyle was an Irishman from Munster, but curiously enough it is the other bible which is printed not in Scots Gaelic but in Erse: O'Domhnull's New Testament, which Robert Kirk edited. Kirk did much to get Gaelic bibles into Highland churches; but he was also a student of the occult and of fairies, and left a manuscript, *The Secret Commonwealth of Elves, Fauns and Fairies* which Sir Walter Scott later edited.

The road along Loch Voil and Loch Doine, in the shadow of the Braes of Balquhidder, bears out all its early promise. It winds and it climbs and descends, often among trees, with a succession of passing places, and because it goes nowhere in particular the traffic on it is relatively sparse and not usually aggressive. The hills beyond the loch are by no means spectacular. They are bare, sometimes with a few trees along their bases, here and there fitfully scratched as by some enormous cat sharpening its claws where foresters have been turning up the soil for planting. Speaking of cats, this is said to be wild-cat country, and the pine marten has been seen on the lochside within memory. The Braes themselves are too near to be easily visible from the road except as big, obtruding shoulders which mask the great hills behind, but the glens which lead up from the lochs give access to some wild and lonely Highland country, the more so with each mile the road winds westwards. Between lochs Voil and Doine is a spit of low, green land sometimes covered by water when the levels are high, and here begins the Monachyle Glen, where more than a half-century ago an ornithologist friend of my father first showed me the golden eagle at close quarters. It was, I remember, a grey day, with the tops all levelled off by a ceiling of weeping cloud, with rarely one of those spectral gleams revealing some scree or corrie high above, and we must have been somewhere under the precipices on the east face of Stob Creagach before a hand caught my elbow, then pointed upwards. In and out of the draggled cloud skirts a bird wheeled. It could have been a raven, but the effortless flight was something I had never seen before. We climbed diagonally, first scree, then steeply-canted slabs and finally among broken crags almost totally hid in the cloud about us. The rock was black, and wet. A fine rain curtained off everything. The only sound was the occasional whisper of the burn a thousand feet below. Quite suddenly we came upon the eyrie where a broad ledge met a cleft in the rock face. It was a loose tangle of heather twigs, filthy with droppings, around it a matted assortment of carrion – grouse-feathers, fragments of fur, the limbs of mountain hares. The stench was sickening. And in the midst of it sat two eaglets, nearly full-grown but with bald patches, and soaked to the skin, the water running down their fiercely-curved beaks and steadily dripping on their talons. Their eyes filmed and unfilmed, but there was no other movement. Anything less regal than the home of this royal bird could not be imagined, and yet the stark realism of it was the perfect climax to the climb.

The heights to the west of the Monachyle are the outliers of a magnificent group of hills. Stob Creagach leads to a wide *cirque* of 'Munros', a Munro being a summit of 3,000 feet or more, the name commemorating the first man to ascend all such summits in Scotland – a considerable achievement as there are 543 of them in all. The highest of this group is Ben More, not far short of the 4,000 feet which in fact is reached only in two small areas of the Highlands. A mile to the south is Stobinian, its western precipices overhanging the head of Glen Inverlochlarig, and close-linked to it is Stob Coire an Lochan. Westwards again there are more Munros stretching to Beinn Chabhair at the head of Glen Lochlarig, and down in this glen, at the point where most of the streams pouring out of those mountains meet to flow into Loch Doine and Loch Voil is Inverlochlarig. It is the location of the house, now gone, where Rob Roy died peacefully in his bed.

From Balquhidder one looks east across Strathyre to the crests of Stuc a Chroin and Ben Vorlich rising above the mass of Meall nan Oighreag. They crown a huge tract of roadless country stretching to the Forest of Glenartney. It is penetrated by a number of glens, but readiest access to the high tops is by the shorter glens striking up from Loch Earn. At Lochearnhead we turn east. There are two choices of road along the lochside. The main road is to the north of the loch, and it has the advantage of affording views of Ben Vorlich; but the south road is another of those narrow, twisting, hilly ways which are much more pleasurable. It turns off the A84 half-a-mile short of Lochearnhead, at a small church, and among trees winds along the hillside about 200 feet above the loch until it crosses the mouth of Glen Ample at the Falls of Edinample. On the hillside below is the castle of Edinample, a Scots Baronial house with lofty towers, once one of the many Breadalbane properties. It is a sixteenth-century structure, one of those compromises between a mansion and a fortress which were still being erected all over Scotland at a time when England was putting up well-fenestrated houses fitted for a more relaxed way of life. Then the road skirts the base of Ben Our and passes through the Ardvorlich policies close to the loch's edge. Ardvorlich itself lies at the mouth of Glen Vorlich. It is the seat of the Stewarts of Ardvorlich, which Scott in *A Legend of Montrose* describes as 'Darlinvarach Castle'. He sketches it, not very precisely, at the beginning of Chapter IV, and later makes it the setting for violent action. Also it happens to be associated with the most celebrated of all Highland charm-stones, that odd group of relics which I have described at length in another book. These stones are rock-crystals of magical repute, used for curing everything from cattle-sickness to the whooping-cough, but sometimes linked with witchcraft. The Ardvorlich stone, known as the Clach-Dearg or Red Stone, is secured with hoops of silver and fitted with a chain. The tale is that it came from the East with the Crusaders but, like others of its kind, it seems to be one of the beautiful quartz crystals which may be come by among the Highland hills, and certainly here on the border of Breadalbane. The *Statistical Account* romantically ascribes the Clach Dearg to the Druids, but more interestingly records that even in the time of the *Account* people all over the district were still resorting to the stone as 'a sovereign remedy in all diseases of cattle'. Glen Vorlich offers what is probably the most direct route for climbing Ben Vorlich. Vorlich is a beautiful hill with a pointed peak which has been described as a miniature Matterhorn, though not on very good grounds. Its crags and deep north-eastern corries are in sombre shade on the brightest day, and from the head of the glen it looks formidable and menacing, but the way to the summit in fact breaks off earlier and follows the northern shoulder.

It is a pretty road along the south shore of the loch, but nowadays in high summer it is littered with tents and caravans, even in the Ardvorlich woods. This of course is something one comes up against all over the Highlands, but the accessibility of Lochearnside and all the quiet roads of the Highland borderland make the problem more acute there. My initial reaction at sight of those caravans is anger at the sheer desecration of lovely country. Then this is tempered at the thought of the deprived millions of an over-urbanised and over-industrialised nation, together with the pricking of a social conscience about a system which has allowed a very few privileged people to monopolise the choicest places. But the conclusion in my mind, I fear, is that the gates to this privilege have been opened too wide too soon. Surely there should be a sharing of this beauty, not the destruction of it which is now in process. The impact of tourism on the Highlands I have already said something about in the introduction to this book, and I will not go over the pros and cons again here; but the recollection of those caravan communities and those red and orange and sky-blue tents polluting the seclusion and peace of this once-entrancing byway underline the need not only for control of the invasion but for some kind of education of invaders who are obviously unaware that their presence in this shape and form is an affront.

St Fillans, the village at the east end of the loch, has always been a popular resort. It is more so than ever now, with its shore made gay by the sails of small yachts and echoing to the sound of outboard motors. Yet it is still an attractive place, and interesting. Curiously, it does not seem to have any direct association with St Fillan himself, the patron saint of Breadalbane, who gave his name to Strath Fillan, 20 miles to the west. But close to it is a celebrated ancient Pictish stronghold: the hill-fort of Dundurn, some distance south of the golf-course and in the shadow of a craggy hill of the same name. Dundurn seems to have been the tribal capital of the

Verturiones, who occupied the province of Fortriu. It is known to have been occupied in the seventh century, but it must have been built many hundreds of years earlier, when the Romans were pushing up northwards from the Antonine Wall. It is positioned to guard the gateway to the hill-fastnesses, or alternatively to launch attacks southwards through Strathearn; and, as O. G. S. Crawford suggests, it is probably because of this that the Romans built a fort at Dalginross, four or five miles down the strath, close to what is now the little town of Comrie. Fortriu, or Fortrenn, has a great area of flat, cultivable land following the Earn eastwards, and together with Angus must have been one of the most populous and flourishing areas occupied by the Picts. There is an impression that 'the Picts and Scots' were nothing more than blue-painted savages waiting to fall upon Britain when the Romans withdrew, but there is no doubt they had their farms and their craftsmen and their townships and most of the other features of an organised community.

Here in Strathearn, with the low lands stretching away eastwards to the distant Tay, and with the peaks of Breadalbane in the opposite direction, we are about midway along the great Highland Border Fault. The broad strath with its fertile fields and pastures and woodlands is part of the belt of Lower Old Red Sandstone which crosses all Scotland diagonally, and the peaks that serrate the north-western horizon, forming the barrier which determined much of the course of Scottish history from the days of Agricola onwards, are massed formations of hard quartzites and schists with some knobs of diorite and granite. It is the existence of the Fault which brings Comrie its reputation as Scotland's, if not Britain's, earthquake centre. Not that this troubles anyone. It is an attractive town, full of trees, and so far as I have noticed little touched by the speculative builder, so that life there on the face of it looks actually more peaceful than the average. The quakes are a reminder that Lowlands and Highlands belong to quite different geological ages, and that the passage of many millions of years has not quite bonded the two. Their occurrences are rare, but some relatively severe shocks are on record. Perhaps the worst was in 1839, when the entire district shuddered and a tremendous

51

subterranean roar was heard, 'like a hundred piece of ordnance discharged at once', and people in the town fainted or ran into the streets and churches were opened for prayer.

The Roman fort at nearby Dalginross is a reminder that Strathearn, or Fortrenn lay in the path of the furthest probe north the Romans ever made on land. There is a chain of their camps and stations more or less within sight of the Stirling-Perth motorway through Strath Allan and the lower part of Strathearn, the line of the actual Roman road passing from east of Innerpeffray to Crossgates. The principal surviving remains of a fort lie about ten miles south of Comrie. The B827 road takes one through pleasant fields for a short while, then crosses the front of Glen Artney and climbs over a wide stretch of moorland holding nothing but a lonely sheep-farm or two and the butts of a shooting-range until the rich fields of Strath Allan unroll ahead backed by the Ochil Hills. Turning right at the Crieff-Braco road, the grounds of Ardoch House are on the left, and the earthworks and ditches of the great camp or fort of Ardoch are easily recognisable although now rough grazing for cattle. It seems really to have been a permanent fort coupled with one or two large marching camps. Sir George Macdonald, once the Grand Old Man among students of Roman Scotland, said that Ardoch 'remains in its decay more impressive than any fort in Scotland', but Crawford qualified this by pointing out that other sites have simply 'decayed' more by reason of farming developments, yet it does appear to have been capable of accommodating up to 40,000 men if one includes the camps, which were in the area where the public road now runs. It survived over a considerable period. Foundations of wooden buildings have been attributed to the time of Agricola, and the later stone buildings to Antoninus. It is thought the Romans gave the name Alauna to it, a name mentioned by Ptolemy and perhaps also associated with the Allan Water flowing close by, as it means 'rocky'. Ardoch is a Gaelic name, *ard* meaning 'high'. There may have been a native fort before the Roman one. There was certainly one on the nearby Grinnan Hill, and there is a legend it is connected to Ardoch by a secret passage hiding treasure:

52

8. *The Monachyle Glen and Stob Creagach*

From the camp of Ardoch
To the Grinnin hill of Keir
Are nine kings' rents
For seven hundred year.

This ancient rhyme once induced a local court to offer his life to a criminal they had condemned if he would descend a deep hole by the praetorium of the camp. He agreed and was let down on a rope. When he was brought up he had with him a collection of Roman helmets and weapons, so the story goes, but on his second descent to find the elusive treasure he died from the foul air. There does appear to have been such a hole until about 1720, but a local sportsman is believed to have filled it in to prevent hares escaping from his dogs.

One could spend a profitable few days at Comrie or Crieff exploring the ground over which the legions passed and repassed in their efforts to inflict a punishing defeat on the ancient Highlanders who constantly threatened them from their mountain strongholds. There was a time when the celebrated battle of Mons Graupius was said to have been fought hereabouts, the critical battle at which Tacitus recorded the defeat of Calgacus and his Caledonians. As stated in the Introduction, this battle must have been fought further north. But Strathearn was obviously of great strategic importance to the Romans. They must have deployed large forces from time to time, what between the garrisons of permanent forts, expeditionary troops in the marching camps and small groups in the chain of signal stations. These last took the form of a raised, circular area with a ditch around it and an inner turf rampart from which a timber look-out tower rose. Macdonald draws attention to towers of this sort on Trajan's Column in Rome, with projecting torch indicating how the signalling was done. There is a signal station at Kaims Castle, just north of Ardoch, there are permanent forts at Strageath near Crieff, at Fendoch and, as already mentioned, at Dalginross. Evidence of the movements of the legions follows a line within sight of the Grampians far away into the north-east; but wisely their generals kept to the low ground and never attempted to penetrate the Central Highlands.

9. The Pass of Killicrankie, Perthshire

CHAPTER TWO

Perth and the North

This chapter-heading may not accurately describe the scope of what follows, but I selected it for its nostalgic ring. Perth is the ancient gateway to the Central Highlands, and when I was a small boy the name had romantic overtones, especially in the mouths of station porters in Edinburgh banging doors as departure time approached. 'Perth and the North!' they chanted above the hiss of steam. The gigantic flickering of the cantilevers of the Forth Bridge brought the next anticipatory thrill, and Glenfarg seemed to be the very doorstep to the hills. But the climax came with grinding brakes as the olive green locomotive and its red-brown coaches snaked slowly into the long main-line platform of Perth station, and everywhere was stir for the change into the strange green Highland Railway coaches, into which they were loading lunch-baskets. Perth in those days was almost a frontier town. The North British and the Caledonian Railways' jurisdiction ended there, and one passed into the keeping of a company whose rolling stock, whose very castellated bridges, had almost a foreign look. For a child it was much more exciting and, I suspect, for adults too. It is all much too easy to-day. The motorway now brings Perth within an hour of Edinburgh, and we can be among the pine-clad foothills around Birnam almost before the day's journey has begun. R. L. Stevenson's wise words, that it is better to travel hopefully than to arrive, are forgotten in this age.

However, the first glimpse of Perth still is impressive enough. The road swerves round a bend, and there is the town spread out below. The setting is splendid – a far rim of blue hills ringing a pleasance of green fields and woods, with the bends of the River

Tay flashing silver in the sun. The town itself has hardly the breath-catching quality of Florence seen from Fiesole, but the river is certainly a nobler sight than the Tiber with which Scott visualised the legionaries comparing it. Yet it is worth remembering there may well have been a signal station somewhere about this point. From it the outposts must have seen the great forts at Grassy Wells and Inchtuthill, and more than one big bridge of timber bound with iron across the broad stream of the Tay – the Tava, as Ptolemy called it – and almost certainly the smoke from a settlement where Perth now lies, for the Romans actually occupied this area for a period covering something like three centuries. They recognised it as one of the most important strategic centres in the country.

Because it has neither castle nor palace a visitor might be pardoned for thinking Perth has played no very important part in subsequent Scottish history. He would therefore be puzzled to learn it is one of the five cities of Scotland whose civic heads are entitled to be called *Lord* Provost; and more, that in precedence it ranks before all the other burghs, except Edinburgh. It is, after all, a town of modest size, with around 40,000 inhabitants. Its early importance stems, no doubt, from its proximity to Scone, traditional place where the Kings of Scotland were crowned, and a number of parliaments were held there. It might in a sense be called the first capital of the country, though one must qualify this by recalling that the earlier Scottish kings moved their courts all over the country; and as to parliaments, the power did not lie in them, but with king or nobles or the church. James I, however, did reside much in Perth, and in 1429 he founded there the great Carthusian monastery, the only one in Scotland, which gives its name to Charterhouse Lane, off King Street. And it was in the Monastery of the Black Friars, also quite gone, that the same king met his death in 1437 at the hand of Sir Robert Graham and a great band of assassins from the north. The tale of Catherine Douglas barring the door with her arm and of the final struggle is well known.

The ancient native name for the town appears to have been Aber-ta, or Tay-mouth, modified to Peart, but in medieval times it

was known as St John's Town – St Johnstoun – and its oldest
surviving building is the Kirk of St John the Baptist, the crown
steeple of which can be seen above the roofs for several miles. Not
that even this may be called medieval, as it was restored in the
nineteenth century. Nave and transept, however, are substantially
thirteenth, and the choir is fifteenth, as the central tower is, and the
vaulting is very beautiful. The church has kept enough of its
character to make it easy to remember that here on 11 May 1559,
Knox thundered forth those denunciations of clerical corruption
which loosed the passions of the 'rascal multitude'. So that here in
St John's the first blow in the battle of the Reformation in Scotland
was struck: not, technically, by a Reformer, but by a priest. Knox
had roused the Perth people by his preaching over several days,
when the unwise priest elected to celebrate Mass and uncovered the
magnificent images on the high altar. A boy protested, and the
priest cuffed him on the ear. The boy's reply was to throw a stone,
which missed the priest and struck the 'glorious tabernacle'. This
began the rioting and the mob seized upon 'the monuments of
idolatry' and, their appetites for destruction roused, proceeded to
the Blackfriars and Carthusian monasteries, leaving only their
shells. It was a sad day for later generations, who in that short time
lost so much of their architectural heritage; but it is a strange fact
that in this same St John's survives the only pre-Reformation plate
in any Scottish church. Exhibited in a glass case are the 'Queen
Mary' and the 'Nuremburg' cups – fine standing cups of silver gilt,
German pieces of Mary Queen of Scots' time – and with them two
handsome London steeple-cups of the reign of Mary's son, James
VI and I. Tradition has it that the ' Mary' cup was found in the
street after the rioting in the church and concealed by a woman in
her father's grave, but Mary herself is unlikely to have been the
donor, as she never visited Perth until after the Reformation broke
in 1560. That the donor might have been her mother, Mary of
Guise, is at least possible. And with those rich pieces in the case is a
superb parcel-gilt silver baptismal basin made by David Gilbert of
Edinburgh near the close of the sixteenth century, one of the
loveliest things which have come down to us from the earlier
Scottish goldsmiths, with the pure lines characteristic of the oldest

church plate of the reformed fashion.

The Perth of Knox's day and before survives mainly in a few ancient place-names, such as Castle Gable. There was at one time a castle, on the St John's side of the High Street, but it seems to have been dismantled as early as 1400. There was even a machicolated city wall, Perth being the only Royal Burgh other than Edinburgh to possess one. The Spey or Spy tower was the main strong point in it, protecting the south gate close to the river, but unhappily this was dismantled at the beginning of the last century. Another building removed no more than a hundred and fifty years ago was the house close to the High Street where the parliaments met. James VI founded a hospital known by his name in 1569, but the present building went up in the eighteenth century, as the original had been destroyed by Cromwell. Cromwell constructed an enormous stronghold on the South Inch, covering 24,000 square yards, which survived the Restoration by no more than three years, surely a record for the dissolution of any building of such bulk. Where the County Buildings now stand in Tay Street, facing the river, the Ruthvens, Earls of Gowrie, had their palace, a town residence to complement their seat of Ruthven Castle, now called Huntingtower, a few miles away. How the town council could have brought themselves to destroy such an historic house is difficult to understand. It was the scene of the notorious 'Gowrie Plot', in which, as it now seems virtually certain, James VI pretended to be decoyed to Perth by the young earl and his brother with murder as the object, in order to have an excuse for killing the two Ruthvens. The wily Jamie feared the power of the Ruthvens, and their enmity – he had had their father executed – and he owed them a matter of £80,000. The citizens of Perth were naturally incensed by the event, the more so as the young earl was their Lord Provost, but the King had a cunning tongue and, from a window of the house, persuaded them to go home. One of the few old houses which has been allowed to survive is that of Catherine Glover, the Fair Maid, immortalised by Scott. It is close to the North Port. Almost inevitably, it has become a shop selling curios and the like.

The prosperity of old Perth ran high, and for centuries it took only a place or two below Edinburgh. There is a nice air of

self-sufficiency in the names of some of the surviving lanes and
back-streets: Meal Vennel, Cutlog Vennel, Horner's Lane,
Skinnergate. But trade and commerce were much more than local
affairs. The Tay is still tidal here, though troubled by sandbanks,
and there was a great deal of intercourse direct with other
countries. Baltic timber came in from the Hansa ports, and logs
were floated down from the Highland hills. The Highlanders must
also have exported quantities of red and roe deer hides through the
town, as the Skinnergate suggests. Salmon fisheries were regulated
as far back as the reign of James I, close season, fishing methods
and all. Tay salmon were certainly as keenly appreciated in the
fifteenth and sixteenth centuries as now. Perth, with the other
Royal Burghs, had the monopoly of exports and cured, salted and
barrelled, at one period only to be paid for with English money or
Gascony wine. There was brisk trade with Holland and Flanders,
channelled through the Scotch Staple at Campveere. All very early
records, unhappily, were removed by Edward I. Traditional
manufactures which have survived to modern times in one form or
another are the textile and dyeing and bleaching industries and
distilling, at one end of the scale, and the fresh-water pearl fisheries
at the other.

Complaints about the destruction of historic old buildings in the
nineteenth century must be tempered by appreciation of what was
built in the same period, because Perth presents a good picture of a
prosperous Scottish country town of around the time of Waterloo.
The main shopping streets of course have had a good many
frontages imposed on the older house-fronts, but invasion by
tawdry modern standard treatments of shop premises so far has
been minimal, and the streets contrive to give the impression of a
survival of good, old-fashioned quality such as has disappeared
from far more famous Scottish shopping thoroughfares, notably
Princes Street in Edinburgh. Tay Street, facing the river and with a
tree-shaded pavement, possesses some handsome public buildings,
but the best houses are in the mellow, vaguely neo–classical
terraces overlooking the North Inch, one of the two historic parks
which are the town's outstanding physical features. Unfortunately
the houses are of soft stone and many of their details have

weathered away. Functionally, they may be out of date, but the façades at least are worth preserving, for without them the Inch, in spite of its fresh green sward and its white-flannelled cricketers in season, would be undefined and certainly less distinguished.

Cricket seems a little out of place in the heart of Pictland, but in fact cricket on the Inches is almost as much a part of the scene as the background of classic grey buildings. Cricket took root in this Highland soil in an odd way as much as a century and a half ago, and it has been said the man responsible for its coming was Napoleon. Many French prisoners were sent to Perth – the present convict prison on the South Inch was built in 1812 to house them – and with them came their guards, who included a Hussar regiment from England. Inevitably the Hussars turned the Inch into a cricket ground and in no time they had converted the local men to the game. Perth, therefore, appears to be the birthplace of cricket in Scotland. Fittingly, the Perth club has an honourable record, counting among its victims not only an All-Scotland eleven but also I Zingari. Before the coming of cricket, however, the two Inches had been the settings for sporting events far back into history. In the later middle ages the usual royal decrees promulgated that frivolous pastimes such as golf and football be 'utterly cried down' to promote more archery practice; but by 1502 it was otherwise, for the exchequer accounts of James IV contain in that year an item: 'To the bowar of Sanct Johnstoune, for golf clubs, xjiiiis.' The sixth James also played golf on the Inches, and has given his name to a golf club which still survives.

In 1396 the North Inch resounded to strokes noisier than bat on ball. There was bitter dispute between two groups of Highlanders said to have belonged to the clans Chattan and Kay. It was agreed – indeed, suggested by the government – to decide the issue by means of a fight between thirty men chosen from each side, the weapons to be the bow, the sword, the dirk, and what was probably the Lochaber axe. A tremendous gallery, which included Robert III and his queen as well as English and foreign nobles, assembled to watch the outcome. Clan Chattan lacked one man and, as Sir Walter tells in *The Fair Maid of Perth*, the town's armourer, Hal o' the Wynd, offered his services. The battle was a dreadful one, drenching the turf in blood, but eventually only a single man of Clan Kay survived, and the eleven Chattan men left were too sorely hurt to follow when he threw himself into the Tay and swam to safety. Although sometimes represented as an illustration of the rather disreputable ways of Highland clans, the battle of the North Inch is now more often accepted as a case of a decision legitimately arrived at under the code of feudal chivalry. The clansmen were merely doing something that was accepted practice in the pages of Froissart's *Chronicles*. And in the Highlands this way of thinking had not died in the eighteenth century.

A page or two back I pictured Perth as belonging to the time of Waterloo, and in spite of its bustling streets – it is a cross-roads from south to north and from west to east, as yet without any by-pass – there is a lingering air of early nineteenth-century values in the quieter corners which is refreshing to experience. Partly, of course, it stems from the fact that so many of its buildings do belong to this time, give or take a decade or two, from the Old Bridge built by Smeaton in 1772 and the barracks of about the same period to the Perth Academy of 1805 and the infirmary of 1836. But also it comes from the tweeds and sprinkling of deerstalkers, the scent of cigar smoke more especially at the time of the world-famous bull-sales, second-hand bookshops where one may still occasionally find a bargain, antique-shops which seem rather less ravished by the wholesale export trade than those further south. It is still possible to imagine John Ruskin playing in the riverside garden over at Bridgend. And speaking of books and authors, there is still a flourishing Literary and Antiquarian Society, which I once had the honour of addressing. It meets in the lecture-hall of the Art Gallery and Museum, a handsome building close to the west end of Smeaton's bridge, housing a small but good collection of paintings and a number of relics, among them a few – all too few – examples of the work of early Perth silversmiths and the Bell of St Fillan, one of the few surviving bells of the old Celtic Church in Scotland.

Scone is across the river from Perth, two miles away on the Blairgowrie road. All Scots school-children know, or should do, that the kings of Scotland were crowned there, but not one in ten thousand could venture a good guess as to why. The Scone ceremony had its origin twelve centuries ago, when Scone became capital of the new combined kingdom of the Picts and Scots. The Scots moved their centre from Dunadd in Dalriada, partly because of the Norse threat, to this Pictish place in Fortrenn, as they moved their religious centre to Dunkeld. The lost rituals of the Scone coronations had their roots deep in the Pictish past, and drew some sort of ancient strength from this. In 1115 Alexander I founded an abbey of Augustinian Canons at Scone, but the sanctity of the place by this time had almost a racial as well as religious meaning. Edward I was nearer to it all than we are. His sacking of the abbey of Scone was no common pillaging, but a search for the token of his enemy's resistance. The most precious possession of the abbey was the Stone of Destiny, supposed to be the receptacle of Scottish strength, like the hair of Samson. Legend had it the Stone was the pillow on which Jacob rested his head when he had his vision, and it was said to have come by way of Spain to Ireland, thence to Dunstaffnage in Dalriada, whence the first king of the united Picts and Scots brought it to Scone about the year 843. The Stone itself, which Edward carried off in 1297 and placed in Westminster Abbey – thereby, according to believers in its legendary power, depositing a Trojan horse in the midst of the Sassenachs – is a piece of the Old Red Sandstone common in Scotland and actually quarried in the neighbourhood of Scone. This may mean anything or nothing. Doubts have been cast on the authenticity of Edward's prize at various times, and after its abduction from Westminster shortly after the war an amusing, learned and persuasive argument against its being the real thing was published by a distinguished archaeologist and former Inspector of Ancient Monuments, the late Dr James Richardson. He compared the quarry-dressed block at Westminster with early medieval accounts of Scottish coronations and with representations on royal seals, and could find no point of correspondence between the plain stone and the royal seats on which the old kings were crowned. In view of Pictish skill in stone-carving and sculpture, it is certainly odd that a relic of such significance should have gone unadorned, and even Henninburgh's account of the stone on which Balliol was crowned at Scone only a

63

few years before Edward's invasion says it was 'hollowed out and fashioned in the manner of a round chair.' Of course, if Kenneth brought it from the west it would not be Pictish; but the Irish were also skilful stone-carvers and much given to adorning significant objects. Whatever the truth, Dr Richardson concluded his essay by suggesting the true Stone was hid away at the approach of the English king, and he remarks it as odd that the Scots showed no enthusiasm when, on two occasions, the English offered to return the relic.

The ultimate destruction of the abbey was at the hand of the mob after Knox's preaching in Perth. The abbot's palace was rebuilt and came into the possession of the Tullibardine family which eventually succeeded to the earldom of Mansfield. The present seat, Scone Palace, dates from the period when so much of Perth was rebuilt, but is in a castellated style. It lies in beautiful grounds, with superb stands of forest trees. The Palace, although built in 1803, incorporates a long gallery where Charles II, on 1 January 1651, was crowned by Argyle, following the ancient Scottish practice since he was hardly in a position to have the ceremony at Westminster. But the Palace's main interest lies in the collections which it houses. There are some historical pieces, among them a bed which James VI owned, the curtains embroidered by his mother, Queen Mary, when she was a prisoner at Lochleven. It is, however, the collection of French decorative art of the eighteenth century which is outstanding. It covers the reigns of both Louis XV and XVI and includes superb furniture of hardwood and kingwood, with many signed pieces, and also the most remarkable assembly of Vernis Martin wares which I can recall seeing anywhere, even in France. Both house and grounds are open to the public during the summer months.

Much as illustrators of romances may like to site their castles on lonely, inaccessible crags, real castles are more often set among the fat lands which can provide a comfortable existence; and as such strongholds drew great events to them, history is made among the hedges and haystacks more often than among the mountains. It is like this in the Highlands. And around Perth, where the hills are low and rolling and unspectacular, it is in the straths that most interest lies. Though it skirts only the outlying foothills of the massed ranges to the north, the Dundee road can provide a long summer afternoon's excursion out of Perth and back. The road follows the Tay, though well above it round the slopes of Kinnoull Hill. On the outskirts of the town is Branklyn Garden, a National Trust for Scotland property which, although only two acres in extent, is well worth a visit especially by anyone devoted to Alpine gardening. Then the landscape opens out a little to a stretch of rich fields and woods, still hemmed in between the river and the spurs of the Sidlaw Hills. This leads into the celebrated Carse of Gowrie. The land holds a rich, open soil made up of alluvium and the weathered sandstone of these parts, but the other secret of its fertility is the shelter from the north afforded by the Sidlaws. Pastures here are more lush, turnips fatter, crops turn golden earlier; and in modern times of course the wise farmer has gone in for soft fruits which find a ready market in the Dundee jam factories. Aggressive as he may have been on occasion, the medieval laird was even more alert than the modern farmer to the advantages of favourable micro-climates, to use the jargon of our times, for he had no short cuts to easier cropping. Consequently, the dens and dells along the south fringe of the Sidlaws are dominated by a succession of castles and noble houses of different periods. What looks like a watch-tower high on the beetling slope of Kinnoull and guarding the Carse is in fact a monument to the admiration which the ninth Earl of Kinnoull felt for the castles on the Rhine, which he observed during a Grand Tour in the eighteenth century. Kinfauns Castle, just beyond this point, is not ancient, and there are many other fine mansions of relatively recent date, but also there are several very old piles hid among the trees to right or left: Megginch, seat of the Drummonds, Fingask, the Tower of Kinnaird. They are not among the great castles, but they are good examples of 'gentlemen's seats' of the fifteenth and sixteenth centuries, erected on their lands with due licence from the king.

Towards the east end of the Carse, on higher ground between Invergowrie and the hills is the little parish kirk of Foulis Easter, a fifteenth-century building of very great interest. It is characteristically simple in design, with little carving, although the lancet windows and the cross on the east gable are pleasing. Its importance lies in the fact that it is still decorated with pre-Reformation devotional paintings. How, so close to Dundee, they escaped destruction by the mob from that town which wrecked Scone Abbey is hard to explain. As late as 1610 we find the synod decreeing that 'the paintrie whilk is upon the pulpitt and ruid laft of Fowlis, being monuments of idolatry, sud be obliterated bi laying it over with green colour'. Three years later things are still as they were, for in a letter to the synod the minister declares that 'my Lord Gray will demolish such of the paintrie as is offensive'. There are some little panels, but the chief work is a big Crucifixion on boards which now hangs on the north wall but originally occupied the area between the 'ruid laft' and the roof. Christ and the two thieves loom sombrely above a crowded scene depicted with considerable detail, but the painting has been cut at top, bottom and sides, giving a slight feeling of constriction. It is a curiously impressive experience in Protestant Scotland, in a tiny village in the Highland borderland, to meet with a Primitive painting of such power, its message concentrated in the scroll issuing from the mouth of one of the soldiers with the words: 'This was the son of God'. Who the painter was we cannot know, but he might have been a Flemish incomer like Van der Goes, whose altarpiece from the demolished Holy Trinity church in Edinburgh now hangs in the National Gallery of Scotland. The first church on the site at Foulis Easter is said to have been built in the twelfth century as token of a lady's hope for her husband's safe return from the Crusades.

Now prosaically known as the A9, the Great North Road out of Perth is like a beckoning hand to all who visit the central Highlands. It is the main route to Inverness and the far north, the only route which strikes with any sort of directness through the mountain mass known vaguely and not very accurately as the Grampians, so it has been the concern of engineers from General Wade in the eighteenth century on. They have straightened so many bends and widened so many cuttings and tempered so many gradients that already it has lost much of its character and interest, and it seems likely to lose much of what is left to speed traffic between Nigg and other North Sea oil developments and the South.

Unhappily the effect on strangers of this 'rationalisation' and 'improved communications' seems to make them more intent on finding how far they can get on their way before lunching than they are on discovering what may lie along the road; but for anyone not pressing north it can be the path to a few days of leisurely exploring.

The first stretch leads uneventfully enough across the upper portion of Strathmore. The plunge into the hills is made with dramatic suddenness: a few climbing curves of the road, a closing-in of forests, and within a few hundred yards the Tay, which has appeared below us to the right, has become a fast, brown Highland river, and the tree-clad slopes to the left rise steep and with rocky outcrops. Indeed, one should realise that the scatter of pines on those crags marks Birnam Hill, location of that sinister wood which in Shakespeare's version of the story spelt the end of Macbeth when they moved to Dunsinane, fifteen miles to the south-east across the Strath. A mile or so past Birnam and the road swings across the Tay, over a handsome Telford bridge of 1809, into the narrow main street of Dunkeld. It is all too easy to press on unawares and miss the real Dunkeld, the sleepy precinct to the west and just beside the river. Old Dunkeld is a model for what can be done with the sort of house which has been condemned as sub-standard and demolished all over Scotland in the past, because this threat hung over Dunkeld until it was rescued by the National Trust and the houses restored by a joint effort of the Trust, which now owns many of them, and Perth County Council. The rather gay frontages, set off by the woods of Stanley Hill, mask comfortable, fully-modernised homes. The scheme has attracted both Saltire Society and Civic Trust awards. This quiet precinct is the perfect introduction to the cathedral, the setting of which with its lawns close by the Tay has been said to be rivalled only by Salisbury's. The Cathedral Church of St Columba is long and narrow in the manner of Dunblane. Part of it, the aisleless choir, serves as the parish church of to-day, but the nave has been roofless and ruined since the Reformation. The choir is in fact the oldest portion of the building, much of it, including a fine arcade along the north wall, being thirteenth-century work, although there has been a great deal of reconstruction. The nave is fifteenth-century. It is on record that even then there was no sort of road to the cathedral and mortar had to be carried in baskets and stones on the backs of horses. The tower is specially notable, its massive buttresses typically Scots, and there is the added interest of some contemporary paintings discovered within the last fifty years, notably a Judgment of Solomon. Dunkeld is a good example of the asymmetrical modifications of the gothic style which the Scots tended to employ, avoiding that regularity which, as one writer has remarked, spoilt some of the finest work in France and England.

There are several tombs worth looking for. One of the handsomest, in the choir, shows a fully-armoured knight with the inscription: *Hic iacet Alexander Senescalus filius Roberti Regis Scotorum et Elizabeth Mare Dominus de Buchan et Dno de qui abit vigesimo quarto die Julii.* The last eight words are restored. This would seem to be the resting place of that son of King Robert II who was know as the Wolf of Badenoch, a lawless character who in the latter half of the fourteenth century carried fire and sword across the Highlands, and whose name we shall meet with again. In the roofless nave is the grave of the last lineal descendant of the Young Pretender, Count Roehenstart, a son of Charlotte, Duchess of Albany, who died in 1854. Dunkeld had various associations with the Pretender, who sent Lochiel and Nairne to proclaim his father king as James VIII from the cross. Of the surviving tombs, however, the best is in the south wall of St Ninian's Chapel: a mitred bishop with his staff, under a canopy. He is Bishop Cardeny, who began the building of the nave in 1406.

As mentioned in passing earlier in this chapter, Dunkeld became the religious centre of Scotland when Kenneth Macalpine united the kingdoms of the Picts and Scots in the ninth century. The transference of authority had actually been affected by his predecessor, Constantine I, but it was confirmed by Kenneth, who brought the relics of St Columba from Iona and built a church to receive them, under a bishop with jurisdiction over the province of Fortrenn. Dunkeld probably was associated with Columban Christianity long before this, as it certainly was a Pictish fortress, because the first part of the name denotes a hill or fort, while the second part seems to point either to the Caledonii or perhaps the Keledei, the Culdees, the 'servants of God', successors to the ancient Celtic Church. Even after it became the mother-church of Scotland, Dunkeld was not safe from the forays of the Vikings, despite its deep seclusion. They were formidable warriors, and some years ago at Uppsala I had the privilege of having Professor Bertil Almgren explain to me just how they were able to take their horses, a small, tough breed, with them in their longships to enable them to make those dreaded lightning-thrusts deep into the countries they landed in. Their first attempt to reach Dunkeld, under Ragner Lodbrog in 845, met with defeat near Clunie at the hand of Macalpine himself with a combined force of Picts and Scots, but in 907 they captured and devastated it. Dunkeld's last threat of invasion, in 1689, was averted. A raw regiment of Cameronians rashly had been ordered to hold it after the Highlanders' success at Killiecrankie, and were almost at once attacked by a force of clansmen four times their number. But the Cameronians were led by possibly the one man Dundee, the victor of Killiecrankie, had feared, the twenty-year-old Colonel William Cleland. The Cameronians fell back on the Cathedral and the mansion of Dunkeld House, now a hotel, and when they had used up their ammunition they ripped the lead from the mansion's roof, drove off the Highlanders and pursued them singing a psalm as they went. Cleland, like Dundee at Killiecrankie, fell in the battle; he is buried in the churchyard.

A few miles up the Tay, at Ballinluig, the Tummel joins the Tay. We shall leave the Great North Road for the time being and keep with the Tay, because it leads into west Perthshire, where there is a great deal to see both scenically and in terms of historical associations. The Tay here comes in from a long valley following the general strike of the rocks, and draws into it an immense drainage system, the outflow of an area of 2,750 square miles, bringing down a greater volume of water than any other British river. Small wonder no other excels it as a salmon stream.

The road follows the left bank of the river by way of Logierait through a succession of fine parklands, crossing the Tay at Grandtully. Few, probably, pause here. A visit to the church of St

Mary's, however, is worth making, although it might be mistaken for nothing more than a low farm building, even behind its scattering of tombstones on the rough grass. It is possibly pre-Reformation, but it was repaired in 1636, when it was given a wooden vault, which is painted. This is quite different in character from the painting at Foulis Easter condemned by the Reformers, being a rather typical piece of Scottish domestic decoration of the period, although Biblical illustrations are inserted in the overall pattern of flowers, fruit and birds. At one time it was the burial place of the Stewart family of Grandtully Castle. The castle is a very good example of what is known as the Z-plan castle of the sixteenth century, with towers at the angles positioned to defend the main building by marksmen shooting through gun-loops. At Grandtully there is a fine staircase-tower which was capped with an ogee roof in 1626, and there is a Victorian addition.

Aberfeldy, some ten or twelve miles up the Tay from its meeting with the Tummel, was like Dunkeld, a centre both of the Picts and of the Culdees, but there are no relics of its more ancient past. Its chief historic monument is the great bridge. With wide central arch and approaches each with two arches, this is quite the best example of all the bridges built by General Wade to keep open military communications in the Highlands. Wade left his mark all over the central Highlands. Despite the fact that he was commander of an army of occupation after the failure of the rising of the 'Fifteen, his work has become part of the Highland landscape, and his memory lingers in a kind of aura of beneficence. By contrast with the uncompromising Cumberland, Wade might almost be represented as the dupe of the people on whom he was supposed to be inflicting military discipline. Instead of carrying out the disarming acts with the harshness with which they were imposed after Culloden, Wade found himself the recipient of vast contributions of rusty, obsolete weapons when all the time well-oiled dirks and broadswords were being concealed in the thatch of their owners' houses. If such weaknesses earn him the indulgence of patriotic Scots, his work as a road and bridge builder turns the feeling into something like affection.

70

10. above *Edzell Castle. 11.* below *Crathes Castle*

Had you seen these roads before they were made
You would lift up your hands and bless General Wade.

For generations this tag was repeated in the Highlands, where the old soldier completed 250 miles of metalled roads of a standard width of 16 feet, and the road-making involved him in building 40 bridges, ranging from monumental structures like Aberfeldy's to quite modest ones spanning burns, all so soundly designed and carried out that some at least, Aberfeldy being one, can carry the heavy motor traffic of to-day without any strengthening. The task began in 1725, and roads and bridges were all completed by 1736. It was summer work only, and very economical, for 500 soldiers were the labourers and they got only sixpence a day in addition to their meagre pay. The resulting communications system, in spite of the forts and bases which supplemented it, seems to have had very little effect on the course of the 'Forty-five rebellion when it came; yet it did help to open up an almost impenetrable country.

Beside the bridge at Aberfeldy is another symbol of that new era in the Highlands: the Black Watch memorial cairn. In this age when the sentiments and traditions of famous Highland regiments seem to be at a discount it is still worth a thought that on this spot beside the Tay in 1739 the first of those regiments was embodied as a regiment of the line in the British Army. Of course, it was all part of the effort to put down and control the Highland 'savages'; but it must be conceded that even as late as the beginning of the eighteenth century there were many among the clans who made uncomfortable neighbours not only for the Lowlanders and Sassenachs to the south but also for sober men north of the Highland line, like Duncan Forbes of Culloden, who felt it was time his countrymen ceased settling disputes with the edge of the sword. The *Freiceadan Dubh*, the Black Watch, got their name because their tartans were sombre by contrast with the *Saighdearn Dearg*, the redcoats of the regular army. They were – and are – the black, blue and green ground of the Campbell, without the yellow or white over-check; and again there is a debt to General Wade, since when the new companies were formed he carefully issued an order in these words: 'Take care to provide a Plaid cloathing and Bonnets in the Highland Dress . . . the Plaid of each Company to be as near as

12. Craigievar Castle, Aberdeenshire

they can of the same sort and colour.' He did of course confuse plaid with tartan. When the companies became the 42nd Regiment of the line, title and tartan were retained, as the Ministry of Defence may care to note to-day. George II made known his interest in the uniform and a 'Searjant and a Centinel' were duly inspected, after which the king commanded they receive 'a handsome gratuity'. The original companies were raised in the Aberfeldy area, and most of the recruits seem to have been tacksmen's sons and sons of landed families, picked for their stature and mien. They believed that their service was to be confined within Scotland, and Duncan Forbes himself, then President of the Court of Session in Edinburgh, made objection when the regiment was ordered to London. All went well until, after a review on Finchley Common by General Wade, these haughty gentlemen of the Black Watch realised that some of the Londoners regarded them as a comic spectacle. Jacobite agents put it about in the regiment that the march south had been merely the first step towards exile in the plantations, and most of the men melted away only to be rounded up and tried for their lives as deserters. Three actually were executed, the rest dispersed among other regiments. It was an inauspicious start; but such battle-honours did they accumulate within the next 75 years that when they came back from the Peninsular War the welcoming crowds in the streets of Edinburgh were so dense that the pipers could not play.

There are two roads to the west from Aberfeldy. One follows the river direct to Loch Tay. In the last couple of miles before we come to the loch the Strath becomes very flat and the river flows in a series of wide bends. There is evidence here of religious rites long pre-dating the Picts, for at Croftmoraig a mound close to the road supports what appears to be be a triple stone circle, concentrically disposed. Some of the stones are quite massive, with a height of eight or nine feet, and the maximum diameter is fifty feet. The river leaves the loch at the village of Kenmore. It is a pleasing village, but with rather a southern look about it, and no doubt was 'created' by the castle, the gothic gateway to which dominates the square, rather as Inveraray was the creation of its castle. Indeed Taymouth Castle, with its towers, may have been modelled on Inveraray. It was built in the first part of the nineteenth century, replacing the sixteenth-century castle of Balloch, seat of Colin Campbell of Glenorchy, which was not very impressive and certainly not grand enough for the Breadalbane family. Queen Victoria came to it in 1842, the year of its completion. She describes her reception, with marshalled Breadalbane Highlanders, pipes playing, guns firing, 'as if a great chieftain in olden feudal times was receiving his sovereign'. There were Highland guards everywhere – on the staircase, standing about in the grounds with drawn swords. She walked to the dairy, 'a kind of Swiss cottage', built of quartz from a neighbouring hill, a brilliant landmark still after more than a century. She tells of the trophies of a shoot in which Albert had taken part laid out on the ground, interesting because they included a wounded capercailzie, a bird which became extinct in Scotland in 1771 and had just been reintroduced by Lord Breadalbane to Taymouth five years before the Queen's visit. One wonders what they did with the wounded bird, but the species multiplied satisfactorily and spread to other parts, although it is nowhere common to-day.

Loch Tay is a flooded valley on an anticlinal axis. It is a long loch, 14 miles, and its greatest width, about a quarter of the way from its east end, is only a mile. It is a very deep loch, over 500 feet, which means that its bottom at the deepest part is something like 160 feet below sea-level. It has not perhaps stirred the romantics as Loch Katrine or Loch Lomond have done, but Robert Burns, Dorothy Wordsworth and Queen Victoria are all agreed about its beauty. This is due not only to far prospects of magnificent mountain groups, but also to more intimate features, wooded dells and tumbling waterfalls. These, as in the case of Loch Earn, make the narrower, winding road along the south side preferable to the first-class northern road, especially as it gives far finer views of hills which include the highest in Perthshire. At Acharn, for example, a short climb takes one to a celebrated waterfall concealed in a wooded cleft at the foot of the glen between Beinn Bhreac and Creag an Sgliata, buttresses of higher hills coming near to the status of Munros. A little further west the loch swings south-west due to a geological fault, a fault which is said to be sensitive to distant earthquakes which are on record as affecting the waters of the loch to the extent of a tidal wave. This is also the deepest part of it. Some of the hills here have mineral deposits, investigation of which was made by the second Marquis of Breadalbane in the intervals of introducing new trees and fauna such as the caper and the American bison, but although he worked some copper and even came on a small quantity of gold, interest in the deposits appears to have died with the Marquis in 1862. But the main pleasure of this road is the simple one of following a track which follows and fits into natural features instead of ignoring and insulting them, so that sometimes there is only a canopy of trees and sometimes a breathtaking panorama of Ben Lawers and Meall nan Tarmachan and Meall Garbh across the water.

At the west end of Loch Tay is Killin, where the Dochart comes down from the great hills around Crianlarich to meet with the Lochay, draining from the Forest of Mamlorn. The Lochay is one of the Highland rivers harnessed to make power, and a complicated system of tunnels and aqueducts helps to promote two power-stations, at Murlagganmore a mile or two up the glen and at Finlarig on Loch Tay. It is interference with the natural flow of water rather than the intrusion of buildings and aqueducts which is the main objection to hydro-electric schemes in the Highlands, but the difference made to the way of life has been enormous. There is still much to do. For crofters living in the shadow of great hills, like those who have their small fields along the north shore of Loch Tay, there are seasons when the hay will simply not dry – and it has been said there is an inch more annually of rain for every mile one goes westwards along the loch! Electric drying could cut crofters' losses dramatically. Finlarig power station takes its name from the ruined castle a short distance away, a castle not only ruinous but threatened further by rank vegetation and perhaps by the roots of the great trees all about it. It was a Campbell seat, associated with the notorious Black Duncan, who made full use of its dungeon and beheading-pit.

Like so many of the higher hills in Scotland, the Ben Lawers massif is deceptively rounded in outline and undramatic in detail, apart from the rugged crags of the Tarmachans above Killin. It is a concentration of Munros, five of them by my count, buttressing Lawers itself, which at 3,984 just fails to achieve the ultimate status in Scottish hills and would probably reach that status if the cairn specially erected 100 years ago had survived. Lawers is in the keeping of the National Trust for Scotland. Geologically, it is a fascinating study, beautifully demonstrated diagramatically by Geikie more than a century ago. I have already said Loch Tay is on an anticlinal axis. Lawers is a synclinal structure. All this simply means is that the folds of the rock-strata here do not present us with the loch in the dip of the folds and the peak where they arch, as one might expect, but the loch has been eroded from an arch and the peak weathered from the neighbouring dip of the folds. The rock from which Lawers is formed is metamorphic schist, which weathers down to a friable soil admixed with small quantities of other materials, sometimes even traces of lime which is a rare element among Highland hills. Here we have the basis of Lawers' reputation as a botanical paradise. Its crags and corries and turfy carpets are jewelled in season with many varieties of campion and saxifrage, especially the saxifrages, including *caespitosa* and the very rare *cernua*, the drooping saxifrage. I say 'in season', but one of the attractions of this kind of garden is that the season varies as one climbs, and plants which have already bloomed at a certain altitude and become blown are in full flower a little higher up. For the more serious botanist, there are mosses and lichens said to be found in no other place in this country. But the National Trust has issued a guidebook to the alpine flora of Lawers – as well as erecting a warning against the removal of plants, which must have happened all too often since the Rev. Hugh MacMillan published his book on the Tay over 70 years ago. Predictably, views from the summit on a clear day are exceptional, from the east coast to the west. Also, there is ample scope for that most rewarding pastime on a still, cloudless summer day, walking the high ridges, and it is possible to scramble around for long periods without ever dropping below the 3,000 ft contour.

To the north of Lawers is a glen of great length, Glen Lyon. Because its road winds for thirty miles and at the end of this merely climbs over a high pass between the hills to return to Glen Lochay and Killin, it is probably not on the itinerary of the average visitor to the Highlands, and it is not the sort of glen which may be sampled from a car window and then away. The approach from the east is by that other road at Aberfeldy, the B846, which turns away from the Tay up Strath Appin, and at Coshieville one takes the side road to Fortingall. Fortingall is noted for two antiquities, both interesting enough although 'exaggerated' in the sense in which Mark Twain referred to the press announcement of his own death. First is the ancient yew in the churchyard, decrepit even when Pennant saw it in 1769 and measured its circumference as 56½ft. Yews are certainly long-lived and this must have survived many centuries of turbulent Highland history, but perhaps not quite the 3,000 years which are claimed for it. The other antiquity continues to be marked boldly on the map as the 'Roman Camp', but this is no more able to be substantiated than the legend that Pontius Pilate was born here. The plan published in Roy's *Military Antiquities* is no doubt what persuaded the map-makers; but Roy never visited the site and O. G. S. Crawford, who did, declares categorically that it is medieval, a moated earthwork, confirmed by the finding of a copper pot in Pennant's time. It seems hardly likely that the Romans would have put a fort in such a vulnerable spot in the heart of their enemies' country. The gate-posts of Glen Lyon proper are two Munros, Carn Mairg and Meall Greigh. This eastward part of the glen is a narrow pass, rocky and with hanging woods, through which the Lyon roars when in spate in a series of falls and cataracts. Dark and rather menacing, this Pass of Lyon is noted for the spot known as MacGregor's Leap, where about 1570 a young man was pursued by Campbell of Glenorchy, the notorious occupant of Finlarig Castle, and for standing in his way was subsequently executed at Kenmore. Thereafter the hills fall back and the woods thin out and there is some cultivated ground, and the most delightful stretch of the glen begins, with some splendid forest trees, including beeches planted early in the eighteenth century, opening up to show views of the great hills ahead. Beyond Bridge of Balgie a little distance there is a two-mile-long avenue of beeches and other trees at Meggernie Castle. Here too there is a vestige of the native pines, the ancient Caledonian Forest, which at one time covered so much of the Highland area. Meggernie is another former Campbell stronghold, built in the sixteenth century, but with its walls rendered white and gleaming in the sun there is nothing at all sinister about it and it is an enhancement of the glen. Beyond this the glen becomes barer and more bleak, and where it winds around the base of Stuchd an Lochain to where the river comes out of Loch Lyon we are back in the domain of hydro-electric schemes.

Glen Lyon is in the heart of Drumalban, the complex of mountains which is the main watershed of the Highlands, with great transverse valley systems shedding rivers to the North Sea and the Atlantic. Penetration usually involves edging this way or that. To reach the next valley northwards we have to return down the length of the glen to Strath Appin and turn left at Coshieville and proceed over the pass to Tummel Bridge. The road skirts Schiehallion, perhaps the shapeliest mountain in the Highlands, its name certainly one of the most euphonious. Its beautiful cone shape is typical of quartzite hills. This hard, whitish rock does not weather down or afford lodgment for soil or peaty deposits, but endures in its stark state, with the minimum cladding of vegetation. But to do justice to Schiehallion one has to get further away from it, and the best prospect along this road does not occur until Loch Tummel is reached, and even then it is necessary to go as far as the so-called 'Queen's View'. From the rock here, at a fair height of over 700 feet, it is possible to see as far as Buchaille Etive above Glencoe and across the Moor of Rannoch. 'Queen's View', however, seems to be a misnomer. It is surprising that even one of the most scholarly recent writers on the Highlands declares it got its name because it so impressed the Queen 'when she visited it in 1866'. In fact, she records in her journal for that year that it was already called the Queen's View when she visited it; and in spite of the day being 'bright' she makes – most unusually – not a single comment on how the view impressed her, but only a complaint about an unsuccessful picnic: 'the fire would not burn, and the kettle would not boil . . . and the tea was not good'. For all that, the Queen's View is worthy of the name.

Loch Rannoch and Loch Tummel are linked in a chain of

hydro-electric power sources with the reservoir created at Pitlochry and given the name of Loch Faskally. It is always unfortunate when any piece of cultivable land in the Highlands has to be inundated to provide power; but from the amenity point of view Loch Faskally has become an asset to Pitlochry, which little village of Victoria's day has grown into a holiday centre of major importance. When the vegetation came to cover its raw edges the reservoir settled down as another Highland loch, and if the great concrete dam rather spoils the illusion, it and its power-house are well-designed and now quite visually acceptable. They are also interesting in themselves and for the salmon ladder, with its viewing-chamber in which the occasional great fish may be seen through the glass darkly battling against the powerful current on its way to the spawning-grounds further up the river – it seems occasional, although several thousand fish ascend every season. And to the north of the town is the trout research establishment, also of concern to anyone aware of the need to keep a watch on what is happening to the fish population of Highland rivers. Another new amenity here – and by new I mean in the years since the end of the war – is the Festival Theatre, which originally performed in an enormous tent, the form of which was perpetuated within a more permanent structure. There is a build-up to a repertoire of six plays every summer season by a professional company. Pitlochry with Moulin, which I remember as a tiny hamlet near which R. L. Stevenson wrote several of his stories, among them *Thrawn Janet,* now looks something of a spa in a bowl of the hills dominated by Ben-y-Vrackie.

Ben-y-Vrackie towers directly above the Pass of Killiecrankie, which by road is a few miles north of Pitlochry. In the days of the old Highland Railway, Killiecrankie was perhaps the most eagerly-awaited point on the way to Inverness. Noses of small boys and girls were pressed to windows almost before the train left Pitlochry station, and eyes peered down through the hanging woods of the gorge to where the waters of the Garry swirled and foamed –

> *Horse and man went down like driftwood,*
> *When the floods are black at yule;*

And their carcases are whirling
In the Garry's deepest pool.

The dramatic scenery of the Pass has probably enhanced the Jacobite victory here in 1689, a victory turned to long-term disaster by the loss of their leader, Dundee, in the first clash. The battle is cited as the classic example of the superiority of the Highlander over regular troops where the terrain is rugged and familiar to him. It also provides two object lessons for the student of war weapons. First, it proved the futility of the old plug bayonet which, in the face of an attacking enemy, had to be jammed into the gun-muzzle after the piece had been discharged, wasting vital seconds. Second, it illustrated the efficiency of the Highland broadsword in skilled hands.

The broadsword may be examined at leisure and in variety on the walls of Blair Castle, at Blair Atholl, five miles to the north. This is the weapon too often mis-named claymore, the claymore or 'great sword' being a two-hander of considerable size, now very rare and much sought after by collectors. The superb blades of the best broadswords were usually forged in Germany or Spain, though they are referred to often as Andria Feraras after an Italian bladesmith whose name was frequently used to proclaim their quality. The basket hilts were made in Scotland, some of the best at Stirling or Glasgow. But there is a large and varied armoury of Highland weapons at Blair, which is the seat of the Duke of Atholl. Among the furniture are some Scottish pieces of exquisite quality, including a pair of cabinets in larchwood veneer by George Bullock. Old as some parts of the castle are – Cumming's Tower was built in the thirteenth century by Comyn of Badenoch – it is specially notable as a museum of Highland relics. Also, it is one of the places noted for the lavish hospitality typical of the Highlander even when it is far beyond his means. It was on the Atholl lands that that extraordinary entertainment took place which Scott describes in *Tales of a Grandfather,* when James V came hunting with a great retinue which included the Papal Legate and the Italian Ambassador. John, the third earl, built for his guests in a quiet meadow a rustic palace with a compartment filled with flowers, a wooden palace defended by wooden towers and surrounded by ponds filled with succulent fish. To the astonishment of the Italians, the Highlanders burned the fantastic structure as the guests departed – a gesture more graceful and extravagant than breaking glasses after a toast! Thirty-five years after, in 1564, Mary Queen of Scots was entertained at Blair. William Barclay, later Professor of Civil Law at Angers University, has left an account of a grand *battue* in which two thousand clansmen drove in the game from Atholl, Badenoch, and even Mar and Moray. The final bag included 360 deer and five wolves. And a number of relics still in the castle call to mind that the same spirit of generous entertainment persisted at the time of Queen Victoria's visit in 1844. Host and hostess greeted the Queen and her husband and the Princess Royal at their door and handed over the castle to them in its entirety for a three-week stay. The comment of the Statistical Account, that Blair may be said to be 'one of the most splendid hunting châteaux in Europe', is no exaggeration.

Three miles on, the road crosses the Bruar Water where it joins the Garry. The triple falls have attracted visitors for centuries, among them Robert Burns in 1787, as a result of which visit he wrote *The Humble Petition of Bruar Water to the Noble Duke of Athole*. In this the stream makes complaint of 'saucy Phoebus' scorching beams', and in the penultimate verse pleads:

> *Let lofty firs, and ashes cool,*
> *My lowly banks o'erspread,*
> *And view, deep-bending in the pool,*
> *Their shadows' wat'ry bed!*
> *Let fragrant birks in woodbine drest*
> *My craggy cliffs adorn;*
> *And, for the little songster's nest,*
> *The close embow'ring thorn.*

The Duke acceded to the petition. The Bruar is well embowered in firs, at least. And now there is another attraction: the Clan Donnachaidh Museum. This pleasant, one-storey building with a flagstaff, designed by an architect who is also a scholar in the field of traditional building styles, is a neat blend of past and present. It is a focus for the great Robertson clan and all its septs, and its location is at the heart of Robertson country, for the chiefs of the clan are descended from the ancient mormaers of Atholl and many of the big houses in these parts, Lude, Faskally and others, are associated with Robertson lairds. But the museum affords a microcosm of clan interests and loyalties in general even for those without the right to wear the scarlet tartan with its deep blue and green over-checks.

The background to all this, in the north, is formed of the big hills of the Forest of Atholl, dominated by Ben-y-Gloe and its neighbours and by Ben Dearg to the west; but the wildness and the grandeur of this country cannot be realised except by penetrating it. This can best be done by going up Glen Tilt, just east of Blair Castle. Glen Tilt splits this mass of mountains and opens the way to an accumulation of Munros, after fifteen miles or so bringing one to a watershed and tracking on to upper Deeside and Braemar. Or a turn westwards where the Geldie Burn comes down leads to Glenfeshie Forest and the backdoor to the Cairngorms, Glen Tilt is not for the easily discouraged – it dismayed Pennant on his pony two centuries ago – but it offers a world which is inaccessible to the slaves of modern means of transport. And indeed from only a couple of miles up the glen there is a splendid prospect up the wide vale of Atholl towards Drumochter and westwards to Glen Errochty, whose waters have been dammed and harnessed to add power to the Tummel-Garry scheme.

CHAPTER THREE

Brechin and Strathmore

There are several main entry roads to Strathmore from the west, two radiating from Perth and two from Dunkeld. I am going to choose the A984 from Dunkeld, leading into the parish of Caputh and at first following the left bank of the Tay, as this is more or less the Roman route into the heart of Pictland, probably followed by Agricola. This is not going to be a Roman pilgrimage. The Pictish remains in Strathmore are more relevant and to me much more interesting than the Roman. But we might pay a last salute to the legions by visiting a very important site, Inchtuthill. It is close to the wide bend of the Tay just before it is joined by the Isla: a curious site, in a way, from the defensive point of view, because it is on what might be called the 'hostile' bank of the river. Like so many Roman remains, it is not too easy to find. It lies south-east of Delvine House and covers a fairly wide area, including a huge square enclosure about 55 acres in extent, with outlying earthworks and a fort, and having traces of a Via Principalis running diagonally from north-west to south-east. Many of the buildings in the forts were of timber, but digs have shown there were also barracks and ramparts in which blocks of a local red sandstone were used, the Gourdie stone used locally in recent times. This all suggests no temporary marching-camp, but a legionary fortress capable of wintering a considerable army. Probably it was occupied for much of the latter part of the first century A.D. Ptolemy names it as Pinnata Castra, literally the winged or feathered camp, but in Roman military parlance the word feathered refers to a kind of rampart. The vulnerability of the fortress to Pictish attacks from the Strathmore side was fully appreciated, and there were extensive

84

defences, the main one an earthwork which now goes by the name of the Cleaven Dyke.

A short distance up the Isla before it joins the Tay is the Bridge of Isla, and close to this are the policies of Meikleour. The house is about a century old, but is not open to the public. It is best known for its beech hedge, which borders the road for nearly 600 yards and reaches a height of between 80 and 90 feet. It was planted in the year of the battle of Culloden – 1746, by Lady Nairne. Meikleour belongs to Lord Lansdowne. A few miles north by west of this is a small piece of water, Loch Clunie, which probably most visitors to the district pass by unthinking; but it is worth a pause, because it contains an island and upon it a little ruined castle which, early in his career, seems to have been owned by that extraordinary wanderer, the Admirable Crichton. He could not have lived there long, because after graduating at St Andrews when most boys are still at school, this youth 'of most beautiful appearance' went off to Paris there to dispute with the learned right across Europe in a dozen languages, to die still young in Mantua about 1585 and thereafter become a legend.

The fertility of the Strath is manifest hereabouts, and so are the benefits of its sheltered climate, shielded from the north by the great Highland Border Barrier, out of the glens of which pour a succession of torrents watering the entire length of the Strath. The floor of the Strath is part of the broad belt of Old Red Sandstone which weathers into the rich soil of these parts, and at first glance some of the fields remind one of a glimpse of Burgundy with its neat vineyards, but with vines replaced by the tall canes of raspberries. The centre and market town is Blairgowrie, twinned by Coupar Angus a short distance to the south, very much agricultural towns both and having nothing of Highland character about them in spite of the fact that the mountains are only a few miles away. Tractors clank through their streets, and populations increase greatly at fruit-picking time. Blairgowrie stands on the Ericht, whose water-power fostered the linen and jute industries from which the town's prosperity mainly sprang. The river has gouged what Geikie called a 'true canyon' in the sandstone north of the town, and the Ericht gorge between Blairgowrie and Bridge of

Cally is not only spectacular but offers an interesting study in rock structures, most of the erosion being through a mass of conglomerate. The Ericht begins only at Bridge of Cally, where it is born of a marriage of the Ardle and Black Waters, typical Highlands streams flowing down Strathardle and Glenshee from the high mountains. There are good roads up both. The Glenshee road connects with Braemar by way of the notorious Devil's Elbow, often impassable in winter; but even winter no longer stops the traffic on this road, which leads to one of the more accessible skiing areas, accessible in the sense that skiiers from as far off as Edinburgh and Glasgow with a mere day to spare can put in a few hours' sport here. It follows, this road, the line of another old Wade road. But it is an ancient route into the north, followed by early Christian missionaries and with its share of legend. The name of the Spital of Glenshee, which produces some levity and puzzlement among visitors, is even on some maps wrongly spelt Spittal, but it derives of course from the hospital or hospice which once refreshed travellers at this lonely spot.

Exploring the Strath means leisurely progress, because the twin roads from the west run parallel for half its length and there are good things strung out along them both. The more northerly, A926, from Blairgowrie, is subjected to further distractions in the long glens penetrating The Mounth and the Braes of Angus, glens which are quite different from other glens in the Highlands, and each offering something different from the others. I am going to take this road first. From Blairgowrie it leads to Alyth, a pleasant town at the foot of a south slope, with the Alyth Burn crossing the main street. This is the border of the Ogilvie country, the homeland of that clan since the twelfth century, and its chief seat is Airlie Castle. A shady road leads from Alyth and winds up the hillside towards the castle, but only the east wall with its portcullis gate remains of 'the Bonnie Hoose o' Airlie' of the ballad, destroyed in 1640 by Argyll, Airlie having fled abroad to avoid signing the Covenant. The Isla river tumbles in a great sweep around the castle, coming down out of Glen Isla from its source far up in the wild country between Glas Maol and its great neighbours where Angus meets Aberdeenshire. Glas Maol, the 'bare grey hill' – a description

86

typical of those heights – has twin summits, one of them in Angus the other over the border, and actually nudges Perthshire as well. Indeed Glas Maol is very close to the Devil's Elbow on the Braemar road, which lies only about 1,500 feet lower. The road goes through the Cairnwell Pass, where in 1602 cattle-rustlers from as far off as Glengarry, with 2,700 head driven before them, were overtaken and heavily punished The astonishing thing is that the regular drove-road from Braemar to the south has a branch which goes right over the summit of Glas Maol itself before following the Isla down to Alyth. Castles such as Airlie and its neighbours must have been useful bases helping to protect the farmers of the Strath from the cattle-raiders descending from the mountains, for the chieftains were their only possible protectors. The writ of the Privy Council did not run beyond the Highland Line.

From Alyth the main road proceeds eastwards to Kirriemuir, but if time is no object the pleasantest way is by Airlie Castle and various winding hillside lanes leading through villages with good Angus names like Bridgend of Lintrathen and Kirkton of Kingoldrum which offer extensive views across the Strath to the south. The prosperity of Kirriemuir is based on its jute manufactures, which a century and a half ago came second only to Dundee's. Kirriemuir has a long history of handloom-weaving; and 200 years ago one of the weavers, David Sands by name, achieved fame by devising a way of weaving double cloth for making stays, as well as a method of making seamless shirts! Yet it is not as Kirriemuir but as 'Thrums' that the town acquired fame in our time, the name given it by Sir James Barrie in his books, because Barrie was born at No 9 Brechin Road in 1860, a house now in the care of the National Trust for Scotland. Here is the 'Window in Thrums', with its far views of the Strath and of the long glens to the north, and of the quaint worlds over the horizon first seen through this modest aperture. The Barrie who took London by storm, the Barrie who tenanted Kensington Gardens with fairies, the Barrie who took his odd cricket-team, the Allahackbarries, to English country houses, seems a far different person from the Barrie of Thrums, the Barrie of the *Auld Licht Idylls,* the Barrie of *Margaret Ogilvy*. But the heart of the matter is maybe to be found in the pages of this last book, about his mother: 'What she had been, what I should be, these were the two great subjects between us in my boyhood, and while we discussed the one we were deciding the other, though neither of us knew it.' He writes there of the click of the shuttle, of the handlooms pushed aside to clear the floor for a dance, but especially of the little girl in a magenta frock who was his mother and in whom all his fantasies had their birth. He came back – and it could not have been otherwise – to be buried in this place.

Kirriemuir, like the other northerly Strath towns, has its long glen going up into the hills, but in this case there are two glens, Prosen and Clova. Where the burn from Prosen joins the South Esk river coming down through Clova is another of the Ogilvie castles, Cortachy. Clova is another of the ancient drove-routes, leading on to Glen Doll and Glen Callater and Braemar, and still a right of way, actually upheld by a court action in 1887. It is only beyond Clova village itself that the track by Glendoll Lodge comes under the shadow of Munros. Here the Gaelic names of the tops are almost non-existent by contrast with Glenisla to the west, and even the great peaks of the border with Aberdeenshire have names like Tolmount and Broad Cairn and Black Hill of Mark, pointing to the fundamental ethnic differences between those living on the Braes of Angus and their neighbours of the Braes of Mar to the north. In Highland parlance those Angus hills have an odd sound, but there may be some Gaelic substructure to them, for after all they were once familiar to the Picts. And a further example of those guardian castles protecting the Strath lies a short distance from the road between Kirriemuir and Cortachy. It is Inverquharity. Also at one time an Ogilvie stronghold, now it is in ruins, but still very striking, still impressive with its nine-foot-thick walls and corbelled tower. Perhaps its most interesting feature is the iron 'yett' (gate) surviving in its entrance. Yetts are rare to-day, partly because they were such effective defences for recalcitrant subjects that in 1606 the Privy Council decreed that apart from those belonging to 'answerable baronis' they were to be turned into plough-irons or the like.

We are now going to double back to Coupar Angus and to follow

13. Daltulich Bridge and the Findhorn River

the A94 route, which parallels, on the south side of the Strath, the previous road. It follows the skirts of the Sidlaw Hills, but its views across the Strath to the Braes of Angus and the mountains beyond are magnificent. The richness of the Strath-lands stands out at almost any season, whether the plough has newly turned up the red tilth or the fields are golden with ripe corn, and because it has been a good place to dwell in since prehistoric times one expects it to be full of interesting remains, and so it is. Angus has innumerable relics from the Stone Age onwards, and is one of the two Scottish areas best endowed with examples of the *souterrain,* or earth-house, one of the best of them at Pitcur, a few miles south of Coupar-Angus. As the name implies, they are underground dwellings, and must have been damp and grim. They belong to the Iron Age, and were no doubt tenanted in the days when Agricola came here. Roman coins and Samian ware have been found in them, also the splendid, enamelled armlets of bronze worn by the Picts. And the monuments of those same gifted Picts, though of a few centuries later, are scattered throughout Angus. Some of the best have been brought together at Meigle, the first village along our road. They are housed in an old school-house, now a museum run by the Department of the Environment. To anyone unfamiliar with Pictish art, it must be something of an experience to get the key from the nearby cottage and let oneself into this former school-room with its strange sculptured stones. Towering above the others is the huge cross-slab listed as No. 2, with its square-armed cross within a nimbus, and on the back of it the arresting representation of Daniel in the Lions' Den, tense with immediacy, the lions and the horses of a group of riders brilliantly depicted. Where did these ancient dwellers in the Strath get their artistry and their ideas? The first they had developed over the centuries, drawing their talents from their Celtic past. Many of their ideas came from far-off places, borrowed from their southern enemies and from peoples they had never met with. This dates probably from the eighth century when the Picts had become Christians, but their pagan heritage is plain in the monsters confronting one another on the shaft of the cross. And at Meigle there are stones with symbols from the earlier pagan period too: the crescent and

91

14. The portrait known as 'The Champion'

compasses, the comb, the mirror, the queer but everywhere consistently-portrayed 'Pictish beast', symbols which may be seen on the backs of No. 1 and No. 4. Archaeologists have been hazarding guesses about their meaning for generations, but as the language of the Picts has not survived it is unlikely we shall ever know for certain what their significance was. The stones at Meigle and the excellent guidebook should be examined carefully, for this will illuminate the monuments on their original sites met with so frequently in the Strath.

Leaving Meigle, we make for Glamis, but a detour by Eassie a little to the south is to be recommended to look at the Pictish cross-slab in the churchyard there. It is a massive piece of local sandstone, 6ft 8ins high, the cross intricately worked with interlace patterns, and beside it twin seraphim (one almost obliterated) with wing whorls linking them with Irish art because they can be matched on the celebrated bronze 'Crucifixion' plaque in the National Museum in Dublin. There are also a tall warrior with spear and shield and, among other animals, an exquisitely-done stag. The back of the stone is less decorative and more damaged, but there are more warriors and what appear to be several bulls, a favourite Celtic motif which we will meet with again away up in Morayshire. A mile or two to the north-east is the village of Glamis – pronounced Glaams. It too comes into the Pictish pilgrimage. Down a lane off the twisting main road are the church and manse, and in the manse garden is a stone of truly massive proportions, almost 9 feet high, with a cross similar to that at Eassie. Indeed, there is yet another only half-a-mile away. These stones show links with the culture of ancient Northumbria, defeated by the Picts at Nechtansmere, which will be heard of again when we arrive at Forfar.

But there is a great deal more to look at in Glamis than Pictish relics. It is an attractive village built of a warm grey sandstone instead of the red so usual in Angus, and rather surprisingly so indifferent to tourists that there is not even a tea-shop in it. Its pleasantest corner is perhaps the lane that leads to the church, with its simple gardens and its background of superb trees – no county in the north grows more splendid forest trees than Angus. The main feature of the lane now is the Angus Folk Museum. It consists of a long row of old cottages run together to form one building, the front being simply decorated with quern-stones and similar things. The museum is a storehouse of byegones relating to the county, ranging from spoons and samplers to a loom symbolic of the industry which supported so many of the towns and villages of Strathmore. Most ambitious of the exhibits are two rooms typical of Angus dwellings of perhaps a century ago. One is a simple cottage interior complete with box-beds, the other a more genteel room furnished with a variety of Victoriana. There are two or three similar museums in Scotland; but the pity is there is not one in every county, or region, for the amount of material being lost annually must be enormous.

The main feature of Glamis is the castle, in spacious park-lands close by the village. It has of course added to its popular attraction because it was the childhood home of Queen Elizabeth the Queen Mother, whose father was the fourteenth Earl of Strathmore, but it is in many ways the epitome of the true Scottish castle before the full impact of the Renaissance and the classical ideas it bore with it changed the nature of these great residences. It is typical, in the first place, of the relationship between castle and environment, for it grows straight out of the park abruptly like an enormous outcrop of rock with no contrived setting of avenues and gardens. No doubt the medieval structure was predominantly of a military nature, and the main surviving portion of this is the central tower; but the greater part of the castle as it exists was reconstructed at the beginning ot the seventeenth century by Patrick, Lord Glamis, who became first Earl of Kinghorne, and he succeeded in changing what may have been a grim enough fortress into a home of great charm. Indeed the third Earl, who became Earl of Strathmore in 1672, kept full particulars of his work in the Book of Record, a manuscript which he wrote himself and which has been a mine of information for historians and writers of after times. Perhaps the most delightful feature of the Record is his repeated apologies for not having recourse to a 'public architect' in designing what he calls his 'reformations'. He says that the 'not-seeking and taking counsell is commonly the cause why things are found amiss in the most part of men's doeings in that way; nor have I the vanity to consider my owne judgement as such as another cannot better.' But it is this natural growth, this organic quality, which makes these northern castles of the seventeenth century what they are. A turret here, a corbelled-out corner there, the bulge of a spiral stair: such things reflect the life and needs of the men and women living inside, reflect the moods and fashions of generation after generation so that the building acquires character and a special sort of beauty as an aging face may do. This, perhaps, is why these castellated Scottish structures often have more appeal than the much grander but more formal French *châteaux* from which they borrow so many of their characteristics. There is no aspect of the old alliance between France and Scotland more visibly manifest than the clustered turrets of the castles in the two countries; but, as the Earl would have said, the French turrets are contrived, the Scots added more 'to please and divert . . . than out of any ostentations.'

The new spirit in castle-building is finely expressed in the Great Hall at Glamis, originally of the fifteenth century. Here we have a barrel-vaulted medieval hall, that rather comfortless centre of baronial life, converted to a drawing-room which almost anticipates the elegance of the eighteenth century. Its crowning glory is the plaster ceiling with moulded ribs and pendants, dated 1621. It is the work of an English plaster-worker who has some other fine ceilings to his credit up in Aberdeenshire, notably at Craigievar. The huge Renaissance fireplace is equally good, above it the monogram of the second Earl and his wife, Margaret Erskine. His son has recorded his pride in and affection for this chamber. A family-group painting of him hangs high on an end wall, presiding over a room which he must have done much to make as it is to-day, for the furnishings belong to his time at the earliest. He completed his university education at St Andrews in the year of the Restoration, and had to set about a private restoration of his own in the castle, which appears to have been stripped of its finery and furnishings in the Royalist cause. Inevitably, he had to employ a good many visiting craftsmen. Among them was the Dutchman, Jacob de Wett, fresh from the marathon contract for the portraits of Scottish kings which still hang in the long gallery of the Palace of

Holyroodhouse in Edinburgh. De Wett's Glamis work, in the chapel, is much more pleasing.

The family name of the Strathmores is Lyon, and they have lived at Glamis for six centuries. The lion motif naturally has its place. It crowns two little pavilions on the roof and in the form of supporters on the beautiful early seventeenth-century sundial in the garden. And there is the famous cup known as the Lion of Glamis, a silver beaker, 'double gilt' and 'holding an English pint of wine', to quote Scott in *Waverley,* who used it as the prototype of the 'Poculum Potatorium' of the Baron of Brawardine, to which he gave the form of a bear. The beaker looks to be a South German piece of the seventeenth century. Among the other precious relics are the sword and watch left by the Chevalier de St George, the 'Old Pretender', who came here during the 'Fifteen, and the buff coat of Claverhouse, otherwise 'Bonnie Dundee'. The castle's association with notable figures in history makes a lengthy list. The chambers known as Duncan's Hall and King Malcolm's Room, linked with Shakespeare's *Macbeth* and with the death of Malcolm II by an assassin's arrow obviously are not of the period, but the tradition has a basis in that Malcolm did die in this locality in 1034 and that 'Lord of Glamis' was the second of the titles which the witches foretold for Macbeth. James V for a long time lived at Glamis with Mary of Lorraine, his wife, and here held his courts after having the widowed Lady Glamis burned at the stake on the Castle Hill of Edinburgh after accusing her of plotting his death, the real reason being the fact she was a Douglas and that her brothers, the Earl of Angus and Sir George Douglas, seem undoubtedly to have been engaged in treasonable scheming. James's daughter Mary, Queen of Scots, visited the castle in 1562. The 'Butcher' Cumberland was an unwelcome guest on his way north to Culloden, and because the family was staunchly Jacobite they dismantled the bed he had slept in. The procession of visitors includes several literary men, Gray in 1765 and Scott a generation later. Scott records experiencing strange sensations. Glamis has its share of ghosts, one of whom is said to have been 'laid' by a visiting clergyman not by exorcism but by a request for a subscription to the church building fund!

Four or five miles on from Glamis, at the east end of a small loch, appears the county town of Forfar. It will seem inconsistent to include Forfar in a book about the Highlands when the city of Dundee is totally excluded, for both at first sight are entirely Lowland in character; but Dundee is cut off behind the Sidlaws and has always been orientated to the outside world, from South Seas whaling and the Indian jute trade to factories with southern and New World backing, whereas Forfar belongs with Strathmore. It is true there is nothing Celtic about Forfar to-day. The speech here has been Braid Scots for many generations, the Lowland group of dialects related to old Northumbria, and in far-off times there were even Frisian settlers in this region, who have left relics of their speech in place-names, especially along the coast. The Vikings too descended on these lands and made forays far inland, although they have left no traces. But the original Pictish inhabitants persisted, and with the Grampian highlands ever present along the northern horizon it is not surprising if there was constant reinforcement coming down out of the long glens – families like the Ogilvies whose castles we have met with on the Braes of Angus, and others such as the Robertsons, Stewarts and Murrays.

As a town, Forfar is not architecturally distinguished. Its core is solidly built of the local stone, made even less distinctive by modern additions. There are no ancient buildings unless one counts the octagonal monument gifted as a Town Cross by Charles II in return for the town's having declared itself for his father during the Civil War. Its prosperity came mainly from the linen and jute which were the staples of so many Angus towns, although the Reid Hall commemorates a once-thriving industry which has disappeared, for its donor made a fortune from a popular sugary sweet known and hawked in the dialect as 'Faarfar Rock'! In the Town Hall are some good portraits by Raeburn and Romney, but perhaps its most locally significant exhibit is the witches' bridle, the gag used to stop those unfortunates from crying out when they were led to execution. Scotland, encouraged by James VI himself, was a happy hunting-ground for persecutors of witches and Forfar was particularly active in this practice which it pursued to a comparatively late date, for in 1661 a citizen by the name of John

Ford was made a freeman of the burgh for his successful witch-detection.

Abour four miles south-east of Forfar, on a road branching left from the A958, is the village of Dunnichen. The derivation of the name seems to be *Dun Nechtan,* meaning the hill or fortress of Nechtan. There is in fact a Hill of Dunnichen, and in spite of quarrying there are still some remains of a Pictish fort on the south side. Irish scribes have recorded for us a battle of 'duin Nechtan'. Old chronicles refer to it as the Battle of the Pool of the Herons, and there are traces of a bog close to the village which had the name of the Mire of Dunnichen. Here, then, we have the site of the Battle of Nechtansmere, one of the most decisive in the early history of Scotland, according to one historian a deliverance greater than that of Bannockburn. Without Nechtansmere there might have been no Scotland, for the Celts would have been forced back into their mountain fastnesses. By the seventh century the power of Northumbria was great and stretched into Lothian and beyond, and after the Synod of Whitby in 662 the power of the Celtic Church was overturned in favour of Rome, the Northumbrians even installing at Abercorn an Anglian cleric with the title of 'Bishop of the Picts'. Ecgfrith, the Northumbrian king, was a man both ambitious and able. Determined to bring the north under his sway, at last he decided on a military invasion and led a huge army north into Pictland, crossing first the Forth then the Tay without meeting resistance. Brude MacBili, High King of the Picts, slowly withdrew before him, then turned on him at Nechtansmere and so completely shattered the Northumbrian army that not even Ecgfrith himself survived. The power of Northumbria did not recover. Pictland won back its territories to the south, the Anglian bishop fled to Whitby. The battle took place on 20 May 685. It is interesting that a Pictish symbol-stone was found on or near the battlefield, and is now in the garden of Dunnichen House. It is rough-hewn or badly shattered, but it carries some boldly-drawn symbols – the so-called 'spectacles', the zig-zag, the mirror and comb. One authority remarks on the wide distribution of those symbol stones as emblems of political unity and suggests that Brude MacBili himself may have been the originator of what may have expressed a national upsurge of feeling after the liberation of the southern Picts. If this is true, the Dunnichen stone should have a very special place among the monuments of Scotland.

Another significant monument lies a mile or two out of Forfar near the B-class road which leads to Brechin. It is Restennet Priory. It has a lofty tower, whose weathered grey and red stones plainly point to great antiquity and closer examination shows it to be early Romanesque, although the octagonal stone spire is much later, probably late fifteenth century. The original part of the priory could actually be a Pictish church, dating back to the conversion from the Irish to the Roman form of Christianity. The climax of the celebrated *Ecclesiastical History* by the Venerable Bede is the chapter in which Nechtan, King of the Picts, asks Abbot Ceolfrid of Wearmouth to send him not only a list of the points of difference in practice between the Roman church and his own but also architects to make a church of stone after the manner of the Romans. St Boniface was the missionary sent by Ceolfrid in the year 710 in response to Nechtan's appeal. We know he came to Restennet after travelling by sea and coming ashore at Invergowrie, and that he paused there before making his way north across the mountains. Did he build the original priory? The ruins as they exist mostly comprise the later, Augustinian house, but parts of the base of the tower could be earlier even than Romanesque. The east archway has voussoirs which seem to belong to Saxon times and the late Ian Hannah saw Irish features in the very narrow south door. This could place the lower part of the tower safely in the eighth century, and Douglas Simpson too accepted this date. It is difficult, then to put aside the exciting conclusion that the hoary stones of this church are a bridge between two epochs in Scottish, and indeed British history. An interesting sidelight on this mission of Boniface's is the sculptured stone in a wall of the church at Invergowrie, where he landed. It may be a few miles outside the region I am dealing with, but it embodies as nothing else perhaps does the actual Romanisation of Pictavia, for it shows three priests, clearly with the Roman form of tonsure of which Boniface makes so much, and with them two of those grotesque monsters which survived from the Picts' pre-Christian past.

About half-way to Brechin the road climbs over the brow of a hill and brings us to the village of Aberlemno. 'Aber' is always a pointer to the Picts in these parts. By the roadside here, close to the stone dyke, are two fine stones. One in particular is impressive, a block of sandstone more than 9ft high standing beyond the dyke, which makes its north side very difficult to photograph. This belongs to the late period of Pictish art, with strong evidence of the impact of continental styles, and Isabel Henderson has pointed out that the mourning angels at the foot of the cross are to be compared with angels adoring Christ on Carolingian ivories, an idea which probably came by way of the Book of Kells school which moved from Iona to Ireland under the Viking threat. On the other side of this cross are some beautifully-executed horses and riders under a group of symbols, the whole so resembling a panel on the Hilton of Cadboll stone, now in the National Museum of Antiquities in Edinburgh but originally in Easter Ross, that the sculptor could well be the same. This is interesting because it shows how unified Pictavia must have been. But there is more to be seen at Aberlemno. The village proper lies down the lane to the south, and here in the kirkyard is another eighth-century cross-slab, also showing marked 'foreign' influence. In this case there are no angels, but the writhing beasts which take their place on either side of the cross are very much in the Northumbrian style of which the supreme example of course is the Lindisfarne Gospels done in the early years of the same century and now in the British Museum. I find it curiously moving to stand in this quiet corner of Angus, with peewits dipping over the fields around, and to see the world of treasures now preserved in London and Dublin and in the Cathedral Treasury of Aachen, Charlemagne's capital, reflected in these carved blocks of local sandstone. And Aberlemno church itself is worth a visit. The original church was dedicated by Bishop de Bernham in 1242, and in the thirteenth and fourteenth centuries it was linked with Restennet Priory. There is little now left that is pre-Reformation, the main survivals being the east and west windows, which appear to have been doorways, and some outside stonework just above ground-level. In 1722 there was radical re-building and the addition of the northern portion.

Episcopalianism has always been strong in the north-east of Scotland, and in the seventeenth century there was something of a tug-of-war over Aberlemno. The minister of the time preferred Episcopacy, but not his congregation, so they removed him by force, but he continued to hold services nearby in Flemington Castle, which he owned. The most precious possessions of the church to-day are the ancient baptismal font of red sandstone, now in the manse garden, and the silver Communion cup gifted by John Ochterlonny, the minister, in 1683 – whose nephew, also John, succeeded his uncle in 1690 and must have been the man ejected for his Episcopacy. The silversmith who made the cup is William Lyndsay of Montrose, who is responsible for the cups of several Angus churches, probably among them the Glamis cups, although they do not carry his punch as the Aberlemno cup does. It is worth mentioning, too, that a stone in the north wall of the church, dated 1604, has the initials J. B. and E. M., representing James Beaton, grandson of Cardinal Beaton, and his wife Elizabeth Menzies. It is thought to have been removed from one of the Cardinal's palaces, Melgund Castle, two miles to the north. One final point of interest at Aberlemno: both small hills overlooking the village, Turin Hill and Finavon, are crowned with early forts, Finavon's being famous. It is of a type first noted in the Highlands, by one John Williams in 1777, and described by Caesar as 'Gallic walls'. They are known to-day as vitrified forts. The dry-built stonework was bonded by timbers, and when the timbers caught fire – perhaps by enemy action, but no doubt deliberately in time – the heat encouraged in the charred wood glowing on those windy hilltops produced with certain sorts of stone a glass-hard mass which greatly added to the strength of the fort. As to the Finavon fort, Douglas Simpson quotes a computation that 250,000 cubic feet of stone and 100,000 of timber would have been necessary to produce the result, and estimates the timber would mean felling 50 acres of woodland. The fort measures approximately 400 by 100 feet.

Five miles along the road is Brechin. The red sandstone of Angus is not a beautiful building stone, and a town like Brechin, which is built of it, at first has a rather grim look, especially on a grey day when the red in the stone does not come to life. Brechin, nevertheless, is a town of some character. The nineteenth century, if it contributed nothing notable, at least built in the same material as the thirteenth, lending a sense of wholeness. But little or nothing of the ancient Brechin has survived, and sadly little or nothing of the archives of documents which once existed, some of which may have been destroyed deliberately by Edward I. There seems to have been a town here by the tenth century, for the Vikings burned it shortly after. In the twelfth century David I probably made it a Royal Burgh, and in the next there was a charter of William the Lyon confirming to the bishops and Culdees of Brechin a right of market on Sundays. Then, in 1296 came Edward, in the person of Bishop Bek of Durham, and on 10 July of that year John Baliol here surrendered to him the crown and kingdom of Scotland, the Great Seal being broken up in the Castle. Seven years later the Castle put up a stout resistance to Edward's forces under its governor, Sir Thomas Maule – it is to-day the seat of the Earl of Dalhousie, head of the Maules. Sir Thomas is said contemptuously to have wiped away with his handkerchief dust from the damage wrought by Edward's 'War-Wolf', his celebrated siege-engine, but it was a stone from this engine which is believed to have slain him on a bastion at the east corner of the Castle wall, probably all that is left of the original structure, for the Castle was rebuilt in 1711.

The beautiful grounds of the Castle flank the road entering Brechin from the west, and descend to the South Esk river, and nearby beyond the moat is the ancient part of the town, the Cathedral with its round tower. There is only one other of those towers in Scotland, at Abernethy in Fife. Such towers are Irish, and the Brechin tower is more purely Irish than is Abernethy, the upper part of which shows Norman influence. The towers were refuges for the clergy in times of invasion by the Northmen, and in the case of Brechin the door is six feet above ground level, making it just that much more difficult to assault. It is 86 feet high, exclusive of the cap, which is later, and of ashlar blocks cut to the circle. Buildings of this kind belong to a period when Celtic tradition had been altered much by the impact of the Continent, but Celtic features persist: windows and door have jambs not vertical but inclined towards one another, and the carving of the Crucifixion above the door is quite foreign to eyes accustomed to Gothic forms, the legs of the Christ hanging uncrossed in the Irish way. The supporting priests too are of the Irish Church, one with the pastoral staff known as the *bachuill,* the other bearing a tau cross. All these centuries after the Synod of Whitby, then, the Culdees were clinging to the vestiges of their insular traditions, and they are Irish traditions, not the Pictish ones which for centuries, as we have seen from the Aberlemno stones, had been wide open to Northumbrian influence. Two weird beasts guarding the door are Irish also. The tower is in fact all that remains of a Culdee monastery, probably founded on a spot hallowed formerly by the Picts, for it was a practice of the ancient church to modify tradition rather than break it. Hector Boece refers to the burning of Brechin shortly after the year 1000, excepting 'a certain round tower built with marvellous art', and one can date the tower as at most a decade or two older than this invasion.

The tower now forms part of the Cathedral, but does not combine too well with it. It may have served as the *cloictech* or bell-tower of the original church, but the present structure had its beginning early in the thirteenth century, and the square tower to the north-west which contrasts with the round tower is the work mainly of Bishop Patrick, who held office from 1351 to 1383. At first sight the Cathedral looks as English as the tower is Irish, but there is a great deal of Scottish detail. The fabric remained relatively intact until 1806, but plainly it was deteriorating and so a great part of the church was reconstructed. Neither the ten altars nor any part of the original woodwork or stained glass remains. In fact, at the 1806 reconstruction it was advocated that the round tower itself should be demolished to provide material for rebuilding, and may only have been saved by the timely threat of Lord Panmure to hang the first man to lay a hand on it! Such conservationist zeal was all too rare then. But fortunately in 1900 some amends were made, even to the taking down of much that had been done in 1806, the ruined choir was given a roof, and as far as possible the ancient appearance was brought back, perhaps the most impressive features being the western doorway and the north-west tower.

From Brechin I suggest taking the minor road which goes north through Little Brechin. After five miles one comes to a pair of hills of just under one thousand feet, the White and the Brown Cathertuns. They are worth climbing for the views not only across the Strath we have been wandering through, but also west to the whole Grampian range, and north across the West Water to the Hill of Wirren and the West Knock, both of them in spite of their modest names rising well over 2,000 feet. The Cathertuns themselves have a name probably of Celtic derivation, which could be either *cader dun* or *caither dun,* that is, fort hill or temple hill. There were prehistoric forts on both hilltops. The White Cathertun, although the stones have collapsed down the hillside, has a certain cyclopian quality. The inner ramparts have been very formidable fortifications, about 25 feet thick at the top and maybe four times as much through the base. Below these are entrenchments and earthworks, with space for encampments. Both fortresses are formidable pieces of engineering. For a long time the ground to the south commanded by the Cathertuns was a traditional location for the battle of Mons Graupius, partly no doubt because it seemed a likely spot, but also because many bones were dug up here, as an old verse records:

> *Between the Killivair and the Bucklie Stane*
> *There lies mony a bluidy bane.*

Following the road past the base of the Cathertuns, one crosses the West Water at the village of Dunlappie and comes to Edzell. Pinewoods fringe the wide, avenue-like road – I recall, as a small boy during the First War, watching women there collecting sphagnum moss for wound-dressings – and then comes a kind of triumphal arch of the local red standstone spanning the way. There is a spacious, pleasant street of modern houses and hotels, as it is a popular resort and a good centre for the district, but the real interest of the place lies in the castle. It is quite easy to pass through Edzell on a fine summer's day in ignorance of this ancient monument only a short distance up the side road on the north of the village. The castle, now preserved by the Department of the Environment, was a seat of that ancient Scoto-Norman family, the Lindsays, family name of the Earls of Crawford, the first of whom was created in 1398; but although the Lindsays were associated with this part of the country from very early, it was only in the sixteenth century that Sir David Lindsay, Lord Edzell, built the castle. It guards the entrance to Glenesk, a Lindsay possession since the fourteenth century when an earlier Sir David married Maria Abernethy, an heiress of the earldom of Angus. Its most arresting feature as one approaches is the Stirling Tower, a keep on the L-plan with a height of about 60 feet. It contains a sizeable baronial hall and its kitchen is of generous proportions and was known as 'the Kitchen of Angus', implying a tradition of hospitality on an appropriate scale. A ruinous building attached to it was added later in the same century, but never completed. However, the most memorable feature of the castle is the work of the son of the ninth Earl. It is the garden, one of the earliest surviving pleasaunces in Scotland. It is well known that the Scots are a race of gardeners, and although many of them won their reputations south of the Border, there are not so many traces of their skill in the north prior to the eighteenth century. The maker of this garden, Sir David, Lord Edzell, as E. H. M. Cox records, anticipated by a century the second Earl of Haddington as the 'Father of Planting' in Scotland, and had a tree-nursery about which correspondence survives referring to 'young birks' (birches) and 'firs and hollins'. The surviving garden here was purely a *viridarium* or flower-garden, and unhappily there is no record of how it was planted, but the Department, which as the Ministry of Works took it over between the wars, has laid it out with lawns and flower-beds which are beautifully kept and form a charming setting for the dark red ruins. And fortunately the walls of the garden itself are not ruinous and have more of interest in them than anything else about the castle. They are divided in compartments three or four paces long, with pigeon-hole recesses for flowers and sculptured stars which derive from the Lindsay arms. There is a delightful little garden-house at one corner, and a succession of bas-reliefs, twenty in all, run round the walls. They represent the Cardinal Virtues, the Liberal Arts and, on the east wall, the Planetary Deities. These sculptures have been identified as copies of a series of copperplate engravings usually attributed to George Pencz of Nuremberg, a pupil of Dürer himself. Lord Edzell is known to have visited Nuremberg, and with a view to investigating possible deposits of precious metals in Glenesk he brought back with him two mining engineers, one of them called Hans Ziegler. Either Ziegler or Lord Edzell himself could well have brought the engravings. The sculptures were no doubt executed by a Scot. The owner's arms and the date 1604 appear above a doorway in the north-east corner. It may be, as one writer suggests, that the heraldic features originally were painted in the appropriate family colours, *argent* and *azure* with the new-cut sandstone providing the *gules;* but there are so many niches and contrivances for flowers in the walls that those could have introduced all the necessary colour.

It is pleasant country beyond Edzell. In a few miles, after the village of Gannachy, the road turns sharp right among trees and crosses the North Esk river. A narrow road opens to the left, passing The Burn, an eighteenth-century mansion where students from the four older Scottish universities may come for reading parties and study-groups and some relaxation. This is the entrance to Glenesk. Glenesk is perhaps the most attractive of the long glens which wind up from Strathmore into the Braes of Angus, not only because of the variety of its scenery but also because of other interesting features. The road follows the North Esk which, although not spectacular, passes through rocky defiles and pine plantations aromatic on a summer afternoon. After several miles river and road alter direction westwards and, climbing through dappled birchwoods, arrive at Tarfside and the Glenesk Folk Museum, which has an importance out of all proportion to its size. It is delightfully placed, with the Water of Tarf tumbling down behind it to join the North Esk. It is the creation of a school-mistress, Miss Michie, and aims to show the byegones of Glenesk itself and all pertaining to it, an extraordinary documentary record of a small community and relatively limited area. I have mentioned the zeal of Lord Edzell and Hans Ziegler to discover deposits of precious metals in the glen, and at Tarfside there are samples of what has been found. Lead ore certainly was present at Invermark, and silver, so often associated with lead, has also been obtained. There were iron-workings and a smelting-house at Dalbog, near The Burn. But this museum ranges also over the natural history and geology of the glen, and it is to be hoped it still offers the rewarding home-baked teas which I remember. After several miles more the glen becomes grander but more remote and unfriendly. Before Loch Lee the good road ends, although a track continues. Here there is another stronghold of the 'Lichtsome Lindsays'. It is Invermark Castle, a typical keep for holding Highland caterans in check, a four-storied tower of granite, now roofless, once defended by a drawbridge. The original tower was built in 1526, but Douglas Simpson detected additions by the Lord Edzell who has been mentioned already. Here again the iron 'yett' has survived. There was of course a drove-road through the glen coming from Ballater and beyond, and a seventeenth-century writer makes it clear that 'Invermark' could swiftly raise levies to deal with cattle thieves. Indeed there was a little community here, and Douglas Simpson draws attention to the fine quality of the carving in the desolate kirkyard, which he associates with the masons who worked at Edzell Castle.

The North Esk was the boundary between the old counties of Forfar and Kincardine. An older name for Kincardine is The Mearns, and if we go east from the foot of Glenesk in a few miles we come into the Howe of the Mearns, which forms the northern end of Strathmore. A howe is of course a hollow place or a narrow plain. The Howe of the Mearns is both: bare but fertile country with small stands of trees sheltering farmsteads, always with glimpses of the Grampian skyline. A bleak, damp wind comes in off the sea at times, and the soil is heavy – I once spent a summer 'clattin neeps' – that is, hoeing turnips – and bigging a vast midden not far from here! It has its own dialect, which is the dialect of Lewis Grassic Gibbon's great trilogy of novels known as the *Scots Quair*, earthy counterblast to the sentimental Kailyaird school the cloying presence of which Scots literature found it hard to shake off. The gaunt, earthier element in Gibbon is more easily identifiable with the seaward side of the Howe, and the long town of Laurencekirk brings me in mind of it, although it can claim fame as fostering a very delicate art. It was renowned for its wooden snuff-boxes. They may seem modest by comparison with the gold-and-enamel trinkets carried by gentlemen of the court of Louis XVI, but in their

15. above *Blackface sheep being driven down from Aberdeenshire hills for shearing.* *16.* below *Loch Ericht and Ben Alder*

way they are as finely made. They are difficult to distinguish from the boxes made in the village of Mauchline in Ayrshire at about the same time: as delicately constructed as a Japanese toy, their characteristic feature the ingenious roll-hinge, working on a wooden pin, so snug it is hard to see how it was made. Sometimes the sheer beauty of the wood is decoration enough, more often a pattern or a picture is drawn or painted on the exterior and protected by a translucent varnish of great purity. More than one firm made those boxes, but chief among them was Charles Stiven and Son, the Christian name of the founder of which was bestowed in memory of Charles Edward himself. They were Jacobite supporters, the Stivens, and their zeal for the cause is reflected in some of their boxes. It was a great snuff-consuming district. Lord Gardenstone was laird, and he himself was a patron of much worth, for he was used to say that if he had a dozen noses he would willingly supply them all with snuff. He is said to have been so lavish with the stuff that the folds of his waistcoat were filled with it, and the villagers helped themselves when talking with him. He was a patron of Stiven, whose establishment survived those of his rivals, and was eventually appointed Boxmaker to Her Majesty. Indeed, the head of the firm himself took his boxes for inspection to Balmoral on the other side of the hills. These beautiful little pieces become rarer every year, and it is hard to come by a good one in the antique shops except at a stiff price. Very often the name of the maker may be found stamped inside the lid. The Stivens, although it is not generally known, had more than a luxury trade. They made a variety of small wooden goods, among them the once-popular toy now known by its name alone: the teetotum. The teetotum was a cube with a stalk on which it could be spun by a twirl of finger and thumb, and 'Stiven's totums' were highly popular with the 'teenagers of a century and more ago, priced at one halfpenny. The stakes in this gambling game, in the Howe of the Mearns at least, were nothing more ruinous than a Yule preen or nut.

'Lawrence Kirk' was on the route selected by Johnson and Boswell when on their tour to the Hebrides in 1773. Johnson had declared himself willing to go two miles out of his way to meet Lord

17. King's College Chapel, Aberdeen

Monboddo, whose house is near the village of Auchenblae.
'Monboddo', Boswell writes, 'is a wretched place, wild and naked,
with a poor old house'. Monboddo, an eccentric, had some points
of similarity to Johnson, but considering the two 'did not love each
other', according to Boswell, the evening passed off tolerably well
and at the end of it the Englishman was in good humour to see his
own black servant, Joseph, riding with Monboddo's black servant,
Gory, as the travellers set off for Aberdeen. At the other end of the
Howe, bringing us back again in the direction of Glenesk, is
another place associated in a sense with Boswell. It is Fettercairn, a
pretty village with an arch resembling Edzell's and a fragment of
Kincardine's town cross. In Fettercairn House lived Boswell's
executor, Sir William Forbes of Pitsligo. And from Fettercairn the
road winds off up into the hills, between the house of Fasque where
William Ewart Gladstone had his honeymoon and which he
retained as his country house and, to the east, a once-royal
residence in Kincardine Castle, a ruin which is all that remains of
the county town. On a fine day this is a superb route across the
hills, cloud-shadows dipping from the hills into the hollows and
mounting again towards the blue-edged horizon to the north. At
Clattering Bridge a narrower road to the right disappears up Strath
Finella which, in spite of the pleasing sound of it takes its name
from the wife of a Mormaer of The Mearns who, in 994, is supposed
to have done to death Kenneth II to avenge his execution of her son.
On such a day it is not a wild place. The final climb to the summit
of the pass of the Cairn o'Mounth – no pass in the ordinary sense of
a defile – brings the reward of a worthwhile panorama. The road at
this point touches 1,488 feet. The place is sometimes mis-spelt
Cairnamount, so losing its real meaning, because the ancient name
of the great barrier cutting Strathmore off from Mar and the rest of
the central Highlands is The Mounth, and many of its summits
underline this, but over the years atlases have dropped the 'h' and
turned Mounth into Mount, a natural enough error. So Mount
Battock, just beyond Glen Dye from the Cairn o'Mounth, should
read Mounth Battock. The Cairn o'Mounth road is the first
through road across the hills east of Glenshee, and although the
other long glens of Angus had their drove-roads the Cairn o'

Mounth seems to have been the main route for the great herds of Highland cattle, and Haldane quotes an account of how the road between Fettercairn and Brechin was blocked for days by thousands of black horned cattle, 'driven by unkempt Celts', on their way to the Trinity Tryst on the Muir of Brechin. Some wild doings must have accompanied this massive traffic through the hills; but through all the centuries before no year can have passed without armed men, either few and stealthy or in hosts with their kings or generals, passing and re-passing by way of the Cairn o' Mounth.

CHAPTER FOUR

Aboyne and Mar

Beyond the summit of the Cairn o' Mounth there is a subtle difference. As soon as the road winds down towards the Water of Freugh and the valley of the Dee one is aware of it. There is rolling moorland, yet when the road falls lower and the moors give way to cultivation again, the country is quite unlike the Howe of the Mearns on the other side of the hills. Streams flow more clearly, more swiftly, stones of cottage and dyke and natural outcrop have a washed hardness and brightness: we have crossed the divide of the great Boundary Fault, crossed from the Old Red Sandstone into a country of metamorphic rocks, granites, a country of glacial drift where the rain sinks swiftly, leaving a drained topsoil which encourages the roots of heather and pine. The air itself has a sharp and yet heady quality, often aromatic with the faint scent of moor plants or ferns or fir-woods. We are in the north.

Deeside merits a chapter to itself because it is not quite like anywhere else in the Highlands. Unlike its rival, Speyside, which it resembles in so many respects, it is not a through-route from south to north plagued by increasingly heavy traffic, but a transverse strath, the only direct access to its upper reaches the notorious Devil's Elbow road which no amount of modernisation has been able to keep open under the worst winter conditions. It has contrived, therefore, to preserve its identity as Speyside has failed to do. Of course, every summer it receives vast numbers of visitors from all over the world, but on the whole they respect it, and in any case, they confine themselves to a few resorts. Deeside is, in a sense, a museum; and like most large museums it keeps some of its most interesting exhibits in corners where they have to be searched out.

112

Deeside as we know it is a sort of glorious folk museum founded rather more than a century ago by an enthusiast with great personal power and influence. Here the genuinely old is blended with a romantic new concept of the past, but the result has every appearance of a going concern, and there is a bloom of prosperity on the strath from end to end which might be envied by regions in the south far richer, materially and statistically. There are no great industries here except the tourist industry, and agriculture is on a very modest scale; but fields are trim, the woods well cared for, houses neat and solidly built, and even among the people one gets the feeling of being on the estate of a prosperous landed proprietor. In short, what incomers there may be do not appear to have taken over yet.

The Water of Feugh joins the Dee at Banchory. With shady woods and a magnificent salmon river like rippling crystal over its pebbly bed, Banchory is a sheltered, pleasant resort, and its clear, dry airs at one time made it a Scottish rival to the Swiss resorts for chest complaints.Yet is is no more than 200 feet above sea-level. Even the hills about it are only a few hundred feet higher. But the valley is so wide here that Banchory is an excellent centre for exploring in all directions, and especially for visiting some of the finest examples of the architectural style known as 'Scots Baronial'. This is a phrase which would be applicable to any castellated structure in Scotland dwelt in by a baron at any time, but normally it applies to the great houses of the sixteenth and seventeenth centuries, in which Renaissance elements from the Continent are brilliantly married to the vernacular style. It applies too to the great crop of Victorian imitations or adaptations in which Deeside is also rich. One of the most beautiful of these castles is a mere two or three miles along the road to Aberdeen. It is Crathes. Crathes embodies most of the features of the style, its setting is typical, it is the seat of a very old family and, not least among its advantages for the visitor it is now the property of the National Trust for Scotland and so open for inspection at regular, stated times. Seen from the garden below, with a stone staircase climbing towards it between dark yews, Crathes Castle is one of the choicest things of its kind in all Scotland. The late sixteenth century tower, severely plain for most of its height, in its topmost third bursts into bartisans and towers and finally chimney-stacks intricately knit together by detail of corbelling and crowsteps and absurd, bristling little stone cannon in place of gargoyles. The stone detail is delicately offset by the texture of the harled walls, that lime rendering of the stone walls applied perhaps mainly for its waterproofing properties but which has a characteristic aesthetic appeal of its own. There is a remarkable unity in Crathes. It may reflect the continuity of occupation by the same distinguished family, the Burnetts of Leys. Originally Burnards, they were of Saxon stock and actually came to Scotland from Bedfordshire before the Norman conquest, a pedigree very unusual north of the Border. Alexander Burnard supported the Bruce in his bid for the throne, and it was in return for this that he received the lands on Deeside. A confirmation of his charter rights issued in 1358 is still shown in the castle. The family did not come to build at Crathes for another two centuries and the house, which took 40 years to build, was completed in 1596. The place was much improved by Thomas, first Baronet of Leys. Then came a long succession of distinguished lawyers and churchmen. Sir Thomas's brother was raised to the bench as Lord Crimond and his son, Gilbert, entered the Church and went into exile in Holland with Charles II but became a friend of William of Orange, so that in 1688 he was created Bishop of Salisbury and Chancellor of the Order of the Garter. His son William went to America and in course of time became Governor of New York, then of Massachusetts and of New Hampshire. A Gilbert Burnett was one of the most eminent Protestant philosophers of his time, holding the chair in this subject first at Basle, then at Montauban. At home, a James Burnett was raised to the bench as the Lord Monboddo whose meeting with Boswell and Johnson had mention near the end of the last chapter.

The Trust has taken over Crathes complete with its furnishings and heirlooms, so that it is as much the perfect example of a Highland castle of its period inside as outside. Even the ancient Horn of Leys hangs above the mantelpiece in the Great Hall, although the horn itself does not form part of the gift to the Trust. Alexander Burnard is said to have been given it, as a symbol of his tenure, by the Bruce when he gave the lands of Crathes in 1323. With its rough stone-vaulted roof and window embrasures, the hall at Crathes is more typical than the hall at Glamis, but the Crathes hall too has lost its medieval air by accumulating an assortment of more comfortable furnishings from later ages. One medieval feature which it shares with Glamis is the listening-hole near the door commonly known as the Laird's Lug, as it was intended to overhear talk of disaffection among the servants or of criticism among the guests. A finer room in some respects is the Long Gallery which spans the entire width of the building. Its ceiling is the original one of oak, with central bosses carved with the Royal Arms in token of the dispensation of justice which was one of the obligations of the laird as tenant-in-chief. It was indeed in this room that the barony courts were held. But the ceiling for which Crathes is most noted is in the Chamber of the Nine Nobles, characters from the medieval minstrels' repertoire depicted on the boards overhead. They are executed in tempera in the style once common in Scotland, of which there is no better example than this at Crathes. Such ceilings unquestionably appear to be native Scottish work, unlike much of the better wood-carving. Closely examined, they are naive to the point of being comical, and by Continental standards crudely carried out; but like many types of Scottish decorative art they are, in spite of their shortcomings, effective and pleasing in general appearance. This Crathes ceiling has the date 1602, and was rediscovered in 1877. In the room known as the Green Lady's Room there is another painted ceiling, but a less impressive one. The Green Lady is a ghost reputed to walk here with a child in her ams, and the tale was at least given substance when men repairing the fireplace about a century ago found the skeleton of a child. The gardens at Crathes also are famous. They date from the early eighteenth century, their yew hedges having been planted in 1702. There are not the sea-borne winter advantages which make possible the exotics found in west-coast gardens like Crarae and Inverewe and Brodick; but there is more summer sunshine here in the east and in a sheltered place like this with its deep, rich soil it is possible to cultivate plants from China and India, from South America and New Zealand. But for sheer loveliness of effect the herbaceous borders and the pool-garden in their seasons are places to linger beside.

Midmar Castle lies north of Banchory, beyond the Hill of Fare, close to the A974. Facing over towards the River Don as it does, strictly it should come into the chapter which follows, but it groups naturally with Crathes and Craigievar. In spite of its situation on a hillside it is not prominent until one is close to it, because it is embowered in great beeches. It is the most massive of the three castles we are now looking at, but there is the same delicacy of detail. Indeed, it seems to be the case that the same school of masons – sometimes called the Midmar school – had a hand in all three and one of them, George Bell, is buried in the kirkyard of Midmar to the north of the main road. Perhaps because it is more château-like in its proportions than its neighbour castles are, French antecedents seem rather more obvious, yet like other vernacular buildings it grows out of the ground and is totally at one with its environment. I am at a loss to understand how Hannah could claim that in sight of the Highlands French forms do not look at home. He may have a case where French masons have been concerned, but here French origins are forgotten and are totally assimiliated. Ancient tradition has it that William Wallace built Midmar, but like the others it is of course late sixteenth century, and the date of death on George Bell's tomb slab is 1575. It belongs to the Gordons of Cluny.

Craigievar is perhaps the most beautiful of this little group. Mr Stewart Cruden in his *The Scottish Castle* says that Craigievar 'as a work of art claims a Scottish place in the front rank of European architecture', and that its front elevations have 'a sort of sublimity'. He describes it as the apotheosis of its type. Its colour is soft and warm, and rising from its surround of sward with its background of dark-shadowed forest trees it is dramatic. It too is tucked away and lies some ten miles or so west of Midmar along the A974, but on a side road, the A980, which leads to Alford. Like Crathes, it is a tower-castle. The simplicity of the lower half like the stem of a plant opens into buds and florets in the shape of clustered turrets and cupolas and balustrades, and the delicate pink harling of the walls leads up to sharply-angled roofs of equally delicate grey. Nowhere is the organic nature of the style seen to better advantage, because like a living thing the tower changes as one walks round it, and again changes if one climbs up among the trees and looks down upon it. The upper storeys are beautifully corbelled out, and at points above the corbel level are sculpted stone heraldic beasts. And the interior is as charming as the exterior. A steep stone stair leads from the flagged entrance, with its yett, to the main chambers on the first floor. The great hall is impressive, dominated by a glorious barrel-vaulted ceiling, the plasterwork of it done by the same man who worked at Glamis a few years earlier. The enormous fireplace supports a stucco panel of the Royal Arms on an even more generous scale. At one end of the chamber is a small musicians' gallery at the height of the panelling. Most other rooms in the castle are small, but the Queen's bedroom, which also has a fine plaster ceiling, accommodates a canopied bed. Unlike Crathes, which has some contemporary furniture, the Craigievar furnishings tend to be of the eighteenth century or later; but there is considerable use of the Forbes tartan, which is of dark green and blue check with a white line. The castle was built by John Mortimer at the beginning of the seventeenth century, but as early as 1610 it was bought by William Forbes, the laird of neighbouring Corse, who had made a fortune by trading with Dantzig out of Aberdeen. Forbes completed the tower and in 1630 his son was created a baronet of Nova Scotia. In 1884 Sir William Forbes of Craigievar became Lord Sempill. The castle is now in the keeping of the National Trust.

Banchory might be called the first gateway to Deeside. The 'gateposts' are the Hill of Fare and the Hill of Goauch, after which the valley narrows, and away on the left beyond the Forest of Birse the tops get higher from Mount Battock to Braid Cairn, and then Mount Keen, first of the Munros in this outlier of the higher hills. Down by the Dee itself and close by there are several pleasant villages, all with the clean-cut granite houses which characterise Deeside. Among the larger is Kincardine o'Neil, where the drovers used to ferry their beasts across the river until 1814, when the fine bridge at Potarch was constructed. A few miles north is Lumphanan, where Macbeth was slain in battle against Malcolm

Canmore, for it was not near Dunsinane, as Shakespeare has it, that he fell. Shakespeare took his story from Holinshed, who passed on the medieval notion that Macbeth was a monster, whereas in fact he was an able enough ruler, and his chief crime was to represent a break in the succession of Scottish kings, an important matter to those trying to defend the Crown from the claims of English kings like Edward I. The next village, Aboyne, is the second gateway to Deeside, and here the hills close in upon the winding river, the heights of Cromar to the north and, across the river, the entrance to Glen Tanner. On the slopes here is preserved one of the few remaining areas of the ancient Caledonian Forest, which at one time covered nearly all the central Highlands. Afforestation to-day means close-planted softwoods, the trees marshalled like the fodder for the factories which they are. Naturalists, probably with justification, wax lyrical about the splendours of the Wood of Caledon. It was a mixed forest, with deciduous trees like oaks supplying the tilth and nourishment for regeneration which the sour carpet of pine needles found in a modern plantation cannot do. There were pines in plenty at the higher, drier levels, notably the true Scots pine with its red bark and deep green foliage. In the depths of this were wolves and boars and bears, and it was the real home of the red deer which now find a much sparser living on the high moors. Destruction of this forest was in part natural, for tree-roots cannot survive changes of climate which encourage the spread of deep mosses; but probably in the main man has been responsible for what has happened, whether Vikings burning out their victims, or iron-smelters, or the irresponsible lumberjacking of huge areas during two World Wars, the gaunt stumps remaining like the gravestones of our heritage. Conservationists such as Fraser Darling have made their pleas for an attempt to re-create those splendid forests, but it is a slow business and may not be possible.

Not many villages in Scotland are built around a village green, but Aboyne is one of the few. The green is the setting for the Aboyne Gathering in the first weeks of September, one of the greatest of the Highland gatherings, to which I will return later in this chapter. In this countryside of castles, Aboyne has more than its share. The Huntly stronghold nearby is an impressive pile, complete with moat, but although its nucleus dates from the seventeenth century the main part was completed in Victorian times. Its predecessor is the castle of Coull, three miles away, a thirteenth-century fortress which as a ruin can still be seen to have been formidable. Aboyne is in no sense a climbing centre – Deeside is not really a rival to Speyside as a gathering-place for truly dedicated mountaineers – but there are several challenging hill-walks leading to the far side of The Mounth. Glen Tanner is a fine glen, and from its head the track known as The Mounth Road leads – if one so chooses – right over the summit of Mount Keen and down into Glen Mark and Glen Esk. The tracks called the Firmounth Road and the Fungle Road through the Forest of Birse meet beyond the Hill of Cat and Mulnabracks, both well over 2,000 feet and descend to Tarfside in Glen Esk. And if one proceeds westwards by the road south of the river, which anyway is much to be preferred to the main road, at the point where it crosses the Pollagach Burn it passes a house on the hillside called Ballaterach, which is where Byron's mother took him in 1796 to convalesce after an attack of scarlet fever. In later life he said it was this visit which gave him his love of mountainous countries; but it was very much a romantic love, a trigger for his emotions rather than something growing out of his store of experience, and his too-often quoted verses on 'dark Lochnagar' suggest distant views rather than the knowledge of 'one who has roved o'er the mountains afar'.

Here at Ballaterach, and across the river at Cambus o'May, the two roads turn the corner into the upper reaches of Deeside. The valley closes in. The heights to the north, Morven and Mona Gowan, now begin to match the hills on the southern side, still dominated by Mount Keen. In a wide bend of the Dee is the chief of Deeside's villages, Ballater, which in high summer grows into a town so far as population is concerned. Its importance until a few years ago derived from its being the terminus of the Deeside railway from Aberdeen, and from early August onward a succession of well-known personalities could be viewed de-training and entering their coaches, later their cars, accompanied by gun-cases and dogs and rods. In this season Ballater became a fashionable resort. It is still popular, but nowhere has the ease and anonymity of car-travel done more to destroy vanity and innocent curiosity than here. Quite apart from this, the Ballater railway was one of those experiences which remained fresh however often they were repeated, and the closing down of an asset with such infinite possibilities was yet another example of control by far-off faceless men without the gift of imagination. It lived for a century. Even the road which goes on to the high hills has suffered the change of perfected gradients and a fine surface; but the Pass of Ballater remains the stern gorge overhung by granite outcrops which has impressed so many newcomers to the Highlands. Geikie made an impassioned plea to the painters of his day to give longer study to the rocks, and he hounds a leading – though unnamed! – Academician for mottling his foregrounds 'with lumps of umber and white', robbing them of both personality and poetry. Nowhere is the bone and character of the face of the earth more marked than in these weathered granites.

Ballater offers ready access to the hills both north and south of the Dee. To the north, at Bridge of Gairn there is a through road up Glen Gairn, which joins the B969 at Gairnshiel. One may follow the B-class road on its spectacular way to the 1800-foot pass between Carn a Bhacain and Mona Gowan, a road which goes down into the head of Strathdon, or away over the formidable Lecht Road, to be mentioned later; or one may follow the Gairn up into the steep recesses between Brown Cow Hill and Culardoch to where the track ends in the shadow of the Cairngorms. But the more varied path to take into the hills is the southern one, up Glen Muick. The main road south of the river is left at Bridgend, near the ruined Knock Castle, a sixteenth-century tower, and the track follows the River Muick in its winding course through pretty birchwoods, which are the policies of the appropriately-named Birkhall on the opposite side of the river. Birkhall was built in 1715, when it had the Gaelic name of *Sterin Stainean*, after the stepping-stones by which the river was forded at this point. It is an unpretentious house of three storeys, with a pleasant air of informality about it which has made it an ideal holiday residence for various members of the Royal Family over the past century. The builder and original owner was Rachel Gordon, tenth laird of Abergeldie, but in 1849 Michael Francis Gordon sold the house to Prince Albert, whose intention it was that it should be the Highland home of the Prince of Wales. The Prince, however, sold it to his mother in 1885. The Queen lent it to various people whom she thought deserving of a stay in her favourite countryside, among them Florence Nightingale when she returned exhausted from the war in the Crimea, and there in the garden the two ladies used to walk together. Inside, as outside, Birkhall is completely informal and looks very much what it was in the first place, the home of a local laird. To return, however, to the road, this comes in a mile or two to the Linn of Muick, a beautiful waterfall. The track leaves the woods behind, and at Lock Muick, it peters out into the simple right-of-way of the Capel Mounth between frowning, bare slopes, on the left the Black Hill of Mark, and on the right Lochnagar itself with its group of great peaks properly designated the White Mounth.

Lochnagar is usually climbed from Glen Callater, beyond Braemar, where the road comes within closer striking distance of the summit; but if a traverse of the mountain is preferred, it is possibly best to approach by Glen Muick, as we have been doing, involving a stiff scramble at the head of the glen, with the easier and shorter run in at the end of the day to whatever transport may be waiting below. Lochnagar of course is not remote in the sense that some of the high tops of the Cairngorms are remote. It is in fact a popular climb, to the extent that there are complaints of a litter problem. Yet on any but the blandest of summer days the prospect of the rock-faces and crags from the shooting-lodge of Allt-na-Guibhsaich, where the Muick is crossed for the ascent to the summit, is impressive. The White Mounth is, as I have said, a group of peaks, all well over 3,000 feet, with Lochnagar the loftiest at 3,786, and in the deep north corrie below is the little lochan which gives the mountain its name. This great granite massif fascinated Queen Victoria. Unlike so many of the poets who have rather inadequately tried to describe it as a feature of the landscape, the little Queen explored it thoroughly and time after time, undaunted by lowering mists. With her husband, she climbed it for the first time in September of 1848 with a keeper from the Invercauld estate as guide, a man of the name of Macdonald. It is worth noting as an example of the Highland tradition of encouraging the lad o' pairts, that Macdonald's eldest son became an attaché in the British Legation in Tokyo. But to return to the hill-top, the Queen got there in a thick, driving mist, in which figures loomed like ghosts. It must be said she had come most of the way on pony-back, but part of the object of the exercise was to enable Albert to do some stalking. He got no stag on this occasion, but bagged a couple of ptarmigan. There are still ptarmigan on Lochnagar. Unlike the grouse, this is very much a bird of the high tops in these latitudes.

Lochnagar is one of the localities from which the Highland jewellery industry obtained its materials, particularly in the nineteenth century. The favourite stone employed is the cairngorm, which takes its name from the mountain of that name between Deeside and Speyside, but Lochnagar, Balmoral and even the Hill of Fare above Banchory seem to have been sources. Cairngorms occur in fissures of granite, crystallising in deep cavities of the finer-grained granites. The prisms may be quite large. The colour ranges from a pale peaty tinge to golden sherry, which is the more highly prized. Quartz is also obtainable in these hills, and very occasionally it is possible on Deeside to find both topaz and purple amethyst. No doubt all such finds become increasingly rare, because the harvest of the long processes of weathering and especially of frost action must soon have been gathered in, stimulated by popular demand. The settings in which the gems were used were brooches, the pommels of dirks and the lids of those great ramshorn snuff-mulls which used to adorn jewellers' windows in Highland resorts. The brooches took the form of the traditional penannular and 'thistle' brooches of ancient times, and were made both for the men's plaids in the Victorian revival of Highland costume and also for catching ladies' shawls. The costume revival was essentially a romantic travesty of the early clansmen's garb, and the use of gems in such settings was in itself entirely wrong; but time sanctifies almost everything, and the travesties which I, among many, roundly upbraided when first I began to write have taken on a sort of antique respectability and command high prices from collectors. One should be wary of the gems. Demand far exceeded supply, and many of those which pass for Scottish cairngorms must in fact have come from Brazil or Russia, but the cost of importing foreign stones has so increased that when they are only semi-precious, like the cairngorm, the profit may not be worth it.

Even on Deeside, horse-brakes have been replaced by shooting-brakes and land-rovers and landed gentlemen move around in conveyances very much like anyone else's, but at least in August and September there lingers here more than anywhere in the Highlands a faint, nostalgic aura of other times which is pleasant to experience although some in the New Scotland think it shame to say so. In the main this is due to the Royal estates which do so much to determine the character of upper Deeside. Three-quarters of a century after, it is astonishing how the joys and, still more, the sorrows of the old Queen survive in this place. The most concentrated evidence of it is in the church of Crathie, bowered in trees where the road makes a great bend around Balmoral. There was a holy place hereabouts in the ninth century. The present church dates only from 1895, but it is well worth a lengthy visit, for its granite walls encompass an epoch. Here in a sense is the heart and core of 'Balmoralism', that extraordinary cult which Queen Victoria fostered in this valley a hundred years ago and the influence of which affected the whole of the Highlands. Not even the Taj Mahal is a more remarkable symbol of a passionate love for a dead partner. The Taj is glorious and perfect, but finite, whereas the memories of the old Queen were translated into a way of life which ended by having a substantial influence on Scotland's social and economic systems. I have said in the introductory chapter that she established a feudal matriarchy and won the sympathy of the Celt; but she also succeeded in changing the attitude of the outside world towards him, until men who had never set foot in the Highlands diligently sought for some shred of right to wear the tartan, that garb of the Gael which Continental propaganda in the time of Gustavus Adolphus had pointed at as a brand of barbarism, and which had actually been proscribed as treasonable less than a century before the Queen was crowned.

Here in Crathie Church is the most intimate sight of the bond which grew between the widowed Queen and those she liked to think of as her fellow parishioners. In this little parish church by the roadside there are memorials to sovereign after sovereign. Beside them are memorials to the men and women up and down the valley. Some of them were well known and loved in the Royal circle: for instance, William Blair, whose stone in the churchyard, 'house carpenter and violinist' as he is described but once known as the Queen's fiddler, one of a long line of Crathie musicians which goes back to John Bruce, said by Burns to have claimed the authorship of 'O, whistle and I'll come to ye, my lad.' And there is, of course, the memorial stone raised by the Queen herself to the memory of John Brown, 'personal attendant and beloved friend', as she says of him on the stone. He was born at Crathienaird and died at Windsor. In an age like ours, morbidly critical of its past, all this smacks of sentimentality, as the granites from Cruachan, Rubislaw and Dyce and the variegated Iona marble of the Communion table are looked upon as in odd taste; but these things are showing lasting qualities which will probably endure longer than the phase of criticism.

Balmoral Castle itself is a notable example of the mode of building adopted by the new landlords of the Victorian age. To shrug off the style as of no architectural consequence, as most critics do to-day, is a confession of pedantry. Any style which perfectly reflects a way of life has significance and is therefore of consequence. The strange proportions, the unsympathetic textures, the pompous exteriors, the cavernous kitchen quarters and chill stone passages – these things are as worthy of study as medieval barbicans and gatehouses. They are symptoms of a different sort of arrogance, of a different sort of contempt for discomfort – qualities which bred the explorers who opened up dark and pestilential areas of the earth with the minimum of support, whatever their motives. There is quality in the building of such places. In a curious kind of way they belong where they are. If their solecisms cause shudders, at least they are committed in no uncertain way, and often they express the laudable enthusiasm of the amateur, as in the case of Balmoral, designed largely by no less an architect than the Prince

Consort himself, if the actual plans were prepared by the City Architect of Aberdeen. The estate at one time was a possession of the earldom of Mar, which lost it in the forfeitures following upon the 'Fifteen rebellion; and the Farquharsons of Inverey, who had the freehold, lost this in the 'Forty-five. The Earl of Fife was the next owner. It was in 1847 that the Prince Consort leased the property, and he bought it a few years after, reminding him as it did of his beloved homeland. In 1852 the purchase was commemorated by a cairn built on Craig Gowan, and the foundation-stone of the new castle was laid on a fine September afternoon in 1853 by Her Majesty. Within two years the castle had been completed, and when the Royal Family entered it an old shoe was thrown after them for good luck. The Prince lived to enjoy it only for a few short years, but they were long enought for the Queen in his constant company to develop a deep attachment to the place, and the national memorial erected to his memory in Kensington is a piece of empty formality when compared with the cairn on the summit of Creag an Lurachain, the inscription on a stone of which carries complete conviction in spite of its hyperbole.

The course of the Dee beyond Balmoral is to my mind best described as stately. The road follows the winding river on its left bank in a series of wide-sweeping curves, the lighter green of the low ground contrasting with the deep green of woods and plantations and with the blues and purples of the mountains, which even late into the summer may be veined here and there with the remains of snow-cornices in the northern corries of Lochnagar and Beinn Bhuird. The country looks what it is, well-cared-for estates marching one with another, the royal lands of Balmoral in the foreground. On the skirts of Lochnagar is Ballochbuie Forest, where again there are relics of the ancient Caledonian Forest, the westering sun glowing red on the bark of the native pines. The buds of those Scots pines are one of the favourite foods of the capercaillie, and although the attempt to reintroduce it here early in the nineteenth century did not succeed, I believe it is spreading again on upper Deeside now. Round the great bend of the river at Ballochbuie begins the neighbour estate of Farquharson of Invercauld, chief of his clan and of its septs, and here the

Invercauld bridge spans the river, erected when the eighteenth-century Old Bridge of Dee was included in the Balmoral Estate, which here occupies the right bank, with Invercauld on the opposite bank. On the hillside above is Invercauld House, seat of the Chief of Clan Farquhar. It is not a very old house, apart from one small vestige of an older tower, but it has been a centre of activity in upper Deeside for perhaps a century and a half. I have a print of 1848, given me by my daughter – the Finlays are a sept of Clan Farquhar! – showing the Braemar Gathering held on the ground before the house. A little further on, in an angle of road and river, is Braemar Castle. It is not a very exciting pile. Built as a 'baronial' tower in 1628, with a round stair-turret in the angle, in 1689 it was burned down, and its present appearance is due largely to rebuilding in 1748, when it became a garrison-point protecting the military road which was being constructed at this time.

Near where the Clunie Water joins the Dee is Braemar. It marks a meeting of ways across the hills. Here the main road comes down to Deeside from the Devil's Elbow and the south, and here too begin the path to the Atholl country through the long, straight reach of Glen Tilt, and also the road and eventually track which follow the Dee itself to its source in the high Cairngorms. Braemar has a place in history from early times, but there is little to show for it. The village's full name is the Castletown of Braemar, which derives from Kindrochit Castle, a hunting lodge of Robert I in the fourteenth century, used also by Robert II a couple of generations later, which stood close to the bridge across the Clunie. Only foundations remain. They have been excavated, but nothing of great value has come from the site except a beautiful silver brooch known as the Kindrochit Brooch, now in the National Museum of Antiquities in Edinburgh. It is of the type known as a 'ring' brooch, and I have described it elsewhere as medieval, carried out in the spirit of the Renaissance, but it dates from the first half of the sixteenth century, which must be shortly before the castle became derelict. On the spot where the Invercauld Arms Hotel now stands the thirty-ninth Earl of Mar raised his standard on the Braes of Mar to launch the rebellion of 1715, proclaiming James III and VIII as King. It was a brave standard of blue worked with the

Scottish arms in gold, adorned with white ribbons, but when the staff was planted in the ground the ball on the top fell off. The small band of followers recalled that when the standard of James' grandfather, Charles I, was unfurled at Nottingham a storm laid it low, and the new omen must have caused deep dismay; but to withdraw was unthinkable, and the Fiery Cross went on its way through the glens summoning the clans in the name of King James. A century and a half or so later a man frail of body but every bit as adventurous as Mar in spirit came to stay briefly in a house in Castleton Terrace. The man was Robert Louis Stevenson. There, at the rate of a chapter a day, he wrote the first nineteen chapters of a book entitled *The Sea Cook,* but which we know better as *Treasure Island.* Perhaps the weather helped its progress, for in an extract from a letter to Edmund Gosse dated August 10 1881, he writes: 'The rain rains and the winds do beat upon the cottage of the late Miss Magregor and of, sir – yours affectionately, Robert Louis Stevenson.'

It is in a park to the west of the village that the most celebrated of all events of its kind takes place in August: the Braemar Gathering. In its present form it dates back to about the beginning of Victoria's reign, and so itself might be claimed as a feature of the legend of Balmoral. How much older than this it is, is hard to say. One tradition credits Malcolm Canmore with its foundation, holding that he offered a purse of gold to the fighting-man who, fully equipped, first got to the summit of Creag Choinnich, the hill behind Braemar Castle. In Victoria's time the Gathering took place on what must have been the old ground, and she describes the event in her diary for 12 September 1850. In that year the race up Creag Choinnich to her delight was won by Duncan, one of her gillies, in under six minutes and a half; but it is recorded that he, like many others, spat blood as a result of the exertion, and so the hill-race was discontinued. Such gatherings were, of course, traditionally tests of strength and of fighting qualities, and it is a pity when the emphasis shifts too far from this. Caber-tossing is still, probably, the climax of the typical gathering, with its premium on a nice mixture of might and skill, but there is a tendency for some gatherings to-day to degenerate into mere athletic meetings, running-strip and all. The Deeside gatherings, however, are setters of standards, and at Braemar the event is very much a Highland one. The Royal Highland Society keeps a jealous eye on what is happening. It has frowned, for example, on the practice of women and girls dancing in kilts, which makes a mockery of so many so-called 'Highland' gatherings both in Scotland and overseas. The kilt is a magnificent dress, but it is an exclusively male dress and so utterly unsuited to the female figure that no discriminating young woman would wear it in a public place; and when participation is turned into a caricature of Highland regimentals complete with rows of tinkling medals won in competitions of the same unhappy sort the result is cheap and nasty enough to flush any real Highlander's face with shame and anger. The same is true of the spectacle of small girls engaging in the sword-dance, so essentially the war dance of the fighting man, like the Maori *haka,* and when the little warrioresses trip around in their ballet-pumps between the crossed blades of a couple of English regimental dress swords supplied by a theatrical agency the last insult is heaped on the injured memory of past glories. The Braemar authorities have laid down the correct garb for women dancers as a simple dress worn with the appropriate tartan shawl or sash, and the better gatherings have followed this example. The Highland gathering is a man's affair, from the lusty piping contest to the dignified presence of the clan chiefs with the tall eagle-feathers in their bonnets, and so it should remain.

With the popularisation of skiing in the Highlands, Braemar has acquired something of a winter season, if not on the scale of the Speyside resorts. It is Aberdeen's access to the slopes of the high hills, other resorts being beyond the barrier of the Cairngorms. For hill-climbing it is an excellent centre, if rather more limited than Speyside or western areas like Glencoe or Torridon. The main route into the Cairngorms is by following the Dee to its source in the great pass of the Lhairig Ghru, but the range of four-thousand foot peaks on both sides of the pass will be dealt with in the chapter on Speyside. Braemar's particular climbing grounds, after the Lochnagar group, are Beinn a Bhuird and its neighbour Ben Avon, which are eastern outliers of the Cairngorms. They are virtually one from the climber's point of view. Seen from further down Deeside they seem to dominate, but from Braemar itself they are obscured by foothills. The foothill in particular is Carn na Drochaide, itself a respectable 2,681 feet, and there is a route following the Slugain burn which suddenly discloses the higher tops looming above Glen Quoich. There may well be snow in the corries of Bheinn a Bhuird even in the fullness of summer: its north top is close to 4,000 feet. Ben Avon is almost as high, but does not look so formidable. The eastern precipices of Bheinn a Bhuird, overhanging the Dubh Lochan, are dangerous when the mists are down.

CHAPTER FIVE

Aberdeen and Donside

Aberdeen may seem to be as much outside the Central Highlands as Dundee is, geographically and ehnically. It is a port, doing much of its business on the seas and beyond them, and is at a considerable distance even from the foothills of the mountains; also it is inhabited by a dour, hard-headed breed of men with no trace of the Celtic temperament. Yet in its way it means as much to the Highlands as Inverness does. It is the doorstep of Deeside, as well as of Donside, and there is a great traffic in and out of it with places far west of Dee and Don, a traffic not alone in the sophisticated things only a large city can deal in, but also in cultural matters, because in higher education it is traditionally Aberdeen that the sons and daughters of ambitious families as far off as the Hebrides have in mind as their first goal – too often, sadly, a stepping-stone to the outer world.

Physically, Aberdeen is largely built of the same stuff as most of the high hills rimming the horizon. To appreciate this to the full one must go out to Rubislaw and gaze down into what must be one of the largest man-made holes in the world. The Rubislaw quarry has, in an inverted sense, all the grandeur of a group of great buildings. Where the buildings soar to the light, it plunges profoundly into the shadows with a dramatic effect few buildings can match. The New York skyline is nothing to it, except perhaps when seen from the Hell-Gate Bridge against an angry sunset. Rubislaw is the work not of a few years, but of centuries. Out of its bowels have come not merely the buildings which, from the Middle Ages to the present, have grown into Aberdeen, but to some extent too the character of the Aberdonians, weathered by their struggle with the sea and the winds that come in with the spume on them. This enduring building material is granite, the granite of the Grampians, and because of it Aberdeen can look like a fragmentation of Lochnagar, especially on a day of sun and rain, when her steeples and pinnacles by turns gloom and glitter against an inky sea and sky.

The historic core of the city is Old Aberdeen, separate from the rest of the city until incorporated in 1891, and the core of Old Aberdeen is the cathedral of St Machar's. It, too, is built of granite: it is the only granite cathedral in this country. No doubt it is the material in part which gives it its uncompromising, militant appearance, and at first sight the almost fortress-like west front has a visage as stern as a helmeted crusader. St Machar's is not quite like any other church, even in Scotland; and yet it is very Scottish. One of its finest features is the great west window, composed of seven tall, narrow lights with trefoil heads. The flanking towers have machicolated parapets, and slot windows only, like castles. Bishop Elphinstone completed a great central tower early in the sixteenth century, but in 1688 it was robbed of its buttresses to build a barracks and it fell down, to the detriment of what must have been a very impressive structure. It is still impressive, far beyond its actual scale. The surviving portion dates mainly from the fifteenth and sixteenth centuries; but maybe its most remarkable surviving feature is the oak ceiling installed by Gavin Dunbar about 1530, a truly medieval concept, not only architecturally but in the spirit in which it is decorated. Its forty-eight shields of arms, gaily painted and gilded, declare the universality of Christendom by displaying the blazons of its princes, among them Pope Leo X and the Holy Roman Emperor, Charles V. It is surely unique that in this building a Presbyterian congregation has worshipped for centuries under the arms of a Pope! Yet this too is characteristic of a city which has always been stubborn and slow in conforming to new patterns. The setting of St Machar's also is very beautiful. Sheltered from the north by parkland trees which hide a loop of the River Don, it faces the Chanonry. As its name records, this used to be the quarter of the canons of the cathedral. Secluded gardens behind high stone walls now surround the houses of some of the professors of the University, the choicest academic residences in Scotland – this, inevitably, is where the late Douglas Simpson lived – and indeed the whole of this part of the town has the air of a precinct, which it has been for several centuries. The Chanonry passes into the High Street of Old Aberdeen, and facing this is King's College. King's, founded in 1494 by Bishop Elphinstone, is built in the form of a quadrangle. Two sides of this are original. One of them incorporates the chapel which, like the namesake college chapel at Cambridge, is the chief glory of the place. There is none of Cambridge's soaring gothic splendour here, yet no college chapel of similar size at Cambridge or Oxford can better it. Indeed, its three-sided apse cannot be paralleled at either English university. Pleasing as the exterior is, the interior is even more interesting, because the professors and students of the University told the Reformers of the sixteenth century that their chapel was their own business, with the result that its medieval state has been preserved with the minimum of interference. There is little enough medieval wood-carving in Scotland left, and King's College Chapel has a high proportion of the total. In the choir are the original superb canopied oak stalls, with pinnacles and lacy tracery and relief work incorporating thistles and the grape-design which is a typical motif of Scottish wood-carving. All this is of date about 1500. The apsidal pulpit is a little later, and was given by Bishop Stewart to the cathedral, from which it was removed.

Old Aberdeen is bounded on the north by the Don. The one-time route northwards out of the town crosses the river by the Auld Brig o' Balgownie, a lovely single-arched bridge with a span of 20 yards, below which the salmon pools are black and swirling. Tradition has connected it with Robert the Bruce, but it seems in fact to have been built by Bishop Cheyn, who accepted the overlordship of Edward I and fled when Bruce rose to power. It is a somewhat impressive structure, with an eerie legend attached to it that one day it will collapse under the weight of 'a wife's ae son, and mear's ae foal,' a legend which used to fascinate Byron as a child and draw him – himself an only son – to lean over the parapet and look into the inky water. So much did the legend haunt him that he came to use it in the Tenth Canto of *Don Juan*. His obsession with being an only son no doubt fixed the legend in his thoughts. Curiously, the great five-arch granite bridge built further down the river about 1830, known as the Bridge of Don, was paid for out of the profits of a small property with which Sir Alexander Hay endowed the Auld Brig o' Balgownie in 1605. Bounded by two rivers as she is, it is not surprising that Aberdeen is well provided with bridges, and the Brig o' Dee, to the south of the city, is in some ways as interesting as the Brig o' Balgownie. It is much larger affair, with seven ribbed arches, and was built around 1520 by bishops Elphinstone and Dunbar. Much of it was reconstructed at the beginning of the eighteenth century, and when, in 1842, the bridge was widened, great care was taken to replace the west face and so to retain the medieval character.

Aberdeen perhaps came as near as any town in Britain to being the independent medieval city-state, although not of course on the extreme Italian model. She was far enough away from the centres of government, whether Perth, Stirling or Edinburgh, to make intervention a protracted business, costly in time and effort. In the fifteenth century therefore, it has been said, she was the most perfect example of an organised Scottish royal burgh. The power of her town council was surpreme. This meant rule through an oligarchy of leading guild burgesses, a somewhat aristocratic body recruited partly from the gentry of the surrounding country. Also freemen of the city, in a more limited way, but jealous of the town council's powers as in other burghs in Scotland, Edinburgh included, were the burgesses of trade, the craftsmen and merchants. They were the real core of independence. The crafts were well organised, and they contributed largely to the pattern of life in the town, with their pageants and feasts, culminating in the procession to St Nicholas' kirk at Candlemas, with an abbot and a prior at its head dubbed the Lords of Bon-Accord. The present east and west churches of St. Nicholas are replacements of the ancient church. Unhappily the work of those early craftsmen of the town has largely disappeared: indeed the medieval heritage of the place is virtually lost, excepting the fabric and some of the furniture of the ancient churches. One might have hoped the die-hard attitude of the citizens would have preserved more! In the burgh records under the date 16 June 1559, the chaplains of the church of St Nicholas urged the provost and town council to safeguard the 'chalices, siluer wark, kaippis (cups) and ornaments' since it was learned that 'certane personis in the southt partis of Scotland hes interpryssit at thair awin hands . . . to distroy kirks . . . and the ornaments and polacie of the same'. Here we have the traditional Aberdonian suspicion of ongoings in other parts. But we find that two years later the precious things had been saved only for disposal to the highest bidder, the money to be 'applyit for the commond weill.' Where the treasures went we do not know.

There are, however, collections of distinction in the museums of the city. One of these is housed in the residence of a one-time provost, Sir George Skene of Rubislaw, an interesting building close to Marischal College. It is one of the very few vernacular buildings outside the Old Town, and was built about the middle of the sixteenth century and modified by Provost Skene rather more than 100 years later. It still possesses some of the original ceilings and mural paintings, and has been turned into a museum of old town life. Skene was one of the numerous body of Aberdonians who, over the centuries, forged a trading link with the Baltic and the Low Countries and through it influenced the way of life of their part of the country. Skene was a very successful Danzig merchant; but men from Aberdeen and the country around founded families in, for example, Sweden. The Swedish House of Nobles has had repeated injections of Aberdeen blood, and their arms are among the many Scots blazons displayed on the walls of that august chamber. I possess myself a replica of one of those great wooden ceremonial Swedish drinking-cups, and it carries the arms of Keith, the Buchan family with a branch in Sweden. The principal art collection in Aberdeen is in the Art Gallery, which also incorporates a regional museum; but the anthropological museum in Marischal College should not be overlooked, because it interprets the subject liberally and throws much light on the life and history of the area.

Marischal College seems to dominate the city from many aspects. The most modern part of the building (1906) fronts an inner quadrangle and is an essay in Perpendicular interpreted through the medium of local granite. Anachronistic though it may be, the impression it produces is a rather splendid one, and the myriad of sharp, clean white pinnacles against the skyline suggests distant prospects of Cambridge or Oxford. There is something peculiarly appropriate in this hard, bright version of gothic. There could be no better symbol of the Aberdonian intellect, with its odd blend of philosophical inquiry with practical good sense – a brand of intellect, it must be admitted, far removed from the intuitive, impulsive approach of the Celtic Highlanders. Dr Alexander John Forsyth, the minister of Belhelvie, who in the early nineteenth century invented the percussion cap for guns, is a good example. But perhaps the man who illustrates it best, in himself and his descendants, is the seventeenth-century citizen David Anderson, known from his ingenuity as 'Davie Do-a'-Things'. He was a mechanic and his virtues were practical; but his daughter Janet, wife of the parson of Drumoak, was the mother of James Gregory, Professor of Mathematics in St Andrews and Edinburgh and inventor of the reflecting telescope, grandmother of a Savilian Professor of Astronomy at Oxford and of another Professor of Mathematics at Edinburgh, and ancestor of Thomas Reid the great opponent in Scotland of the scepticism of David Hume. Reid himself was a graduate and librarian of Marischal College.

We are concerned with Aberdeen purely as the granite doorstep of the Highlands to the east, so that its problems of to-day are relevant only in so far as they affect the Highlands, but there is no doubt that the tens of thousands of tourists who every summer stop here on their way to Braemar will find a changing city as the years go by. The main reason is that Aberdeen no longer harvests from the North Sea fish alone, but has become the main shore terminal of the complex of deep-sea oil-fields. It is not so much bringing the pipelines ashore which will alter the city and its near vicinity, but the build-up of platform services and the growth of all kinds of ancillary industries which may change completely the character of the place. The colony of Texan oil-experts no doubt will disappear in time and much of the construction work which has been used so speciously as an argument for long-term prosperity will vanish too;

but will the taste of big-time industrial rapacity and the seduction of pay-packets far beyond the familiar scales leave the people as they were traditionally any more than they will leave the face of city and country unscarred? The retort that one cannot stop progress is now a recognisably hollow one: the atom-bomb at least did that for us. I have raised the whole question of 'progress' in the Highlands in the introductory chapter and tried to weigh the need for real development against mere exploitation, but Aberdeen is perhaps the place where the Highland economy and outlook come nearest to confronting in a big way what is going on in the rest of the country. Here, in a city which has fed back to the glens and islands as teachers so many of those young men and women who came to her for training, the sound values which so many of them brought with them can either be reinforced or rudely changed. I know there are some who think this attitude is romantic poppycock, that the Highlander is no better and no worse than his counterpart in the outside world; but at least his high hills and his transport problems still tend to render him that much different, and I believe there is a good case for keeping it that way.

Even in its higher reaches the course of the Don is much less spectacular than the Dee's. The Dee's bed is in granite, the Don's in loam. It may be argued the Don is not a Highland river at all, except in its upper reaches; yet even if there is not one Munro draining into it the whole way to its source there are cultural and historical bonds which link it with the Highlands, and I believe one must penetrate into Buchan before the Highlands are left behind. The clans of Gordon, for example, can be traced in a wide arc all the way from Speyside to Aberdeen. Strathbogie is the heartland of this territory, and there the chiefship is located, but the Marquess of Aberdeen far east at Haddo is descended from a Gordon, and Aberdeen itself is bound up with the clan in many ways, from the name of Robert Gordon's College, founded by the first graduate of Marischal College, to the regiment of the Gordon Highlanders, whose headquarters are in the city. But the eastern segment of this arc, which is roughly what this chapter is about, is mellower than the high country to the west. It has been congenial to man for much longer, for one may dig deeper into its soil before striking rock, and its fields and villages feel ripe and lived-in. It has castles greater, although not more choice, than Deeside's, but there are many more modest signs of a long-lasting prosperity. One of these is the endowment of the churches in the larger villages. Several of these churches possess fine silver Communion cups dating from the seventeenth century, and it is interesting that most of the Donside cups are in a style found almost exclusively in the north-east of Scotland. It is beaker-shaped, this type of cup, and is one of the things which remind us of Aberdeenshire's link with the Continent, especially the Low Countries. King's College in Aberdeen and also St Machar's have beautiful foreign-made cups in this style, finely engraved, presented by foreign students, and the parish church in the village of Ellon is the fortunate owner of a pair of beaker cups one of which carries the Amsterdam hall-mark and the other the punch of Walter Melvil, an Aberdeen silversmith. Fintry, on the Don, has a pair closely resembling the Ellon cups and obviously copied from them. Monymusk, a secluded village beside the river just where it begins to wind into the Grampian foothills, has no fewer than four such cups. They carry the date 1691, and the initials of the minister of that day, John Burnett. The kirk session records show they cost £125 2s.

The church at Monymusk is interesting in itself, as part of the fabric of the Romanesque church survives in it; but there was a Culdee settlement here, and at Abersnithack just across the Don it is possible to detect the outline of a little chapel which may have been ministered to by St Finan, one of the disciples of St Kentigern in his mission to the Picts. Kentigern came from what is now St Asaph's in North Wales. It is interesting that the disciples have left their names on church sites both in Anglesey and hereabouts in Aberdeenshire. What may be evidence of the success of Kentigern's mission is a stone preserved at Monymusk House on which a characteristic Pictish cross is depicted. This fifteenth-century house also at one time sheltered what is in some respects the most notable of Scotland's national relics: the Brecbennoch of St Columba, otherwise known as the Monymusk Reliquary. This precious box cased in bronze and silver is now preserved in the National Museum of Antiquities. It is supposed to have held the Psalter of

137

Columba. Undoubtedly the Scots people regarded it as a sort of palladium, for it was called the Cathach, or shrine, or the Battler, and Adamnan records that if it is sent thrice sunways round the army of Columba's clan, the Cinel Conall Gulban, they will return from battle victorious. The reliquary can be dated to about A.D. 700, and may well have been associated with the transfer of Columba's relics from Iona to Dunkeld; but the first certain knowledge of it is its deposition in Arbroath Abbey at the beginning of the thirteenth century. It seems the Abbot of Arbroath invoked its powers by carrying it at the battle of Bannockburn. In 1415 it came to Monymusk and apart from a period with the Irvines of Drum it remained there until 1923, when the museum bought it from the Grants of Monymusk. It is a characteristic 'hip-roofed' shrine of the old Irish church, some of which can be seen among Viking loot in Scandinavian museums.

The entire area north of the great bend which the Don takes between Inverurie and Monymusk is filled with things of anti-quarian interest. There are several Pictish stones in the kirkyard at Inverurie, a royal burgh located at the point where the Urie flows into the Don, and if one follows this tributary a few miles up to Chapel of Garioch there is by the roadside one of the tallest of Pictish monuments, the Maiden Stone, apparently so-called because the familiar mirror and comb are among the symbols carved on it. On the other side is a cross, so this stone too marks a consecrated site, which may also explain the name of the village. Superstition and legend have accumulated around the stone, but the story associated with its name is about a young beauty known as the Maiden of Drumdurno. This girl was baking cakes before her wedding, to take place on the following day, when a handsome stranger wagered he could lay a stone 'causey' (causeway) right to the highest point, the Mither Tap, of the nearby hill of Bennachie before she had finished her baking, the prize to be her heart. She lightly agreed to what she thought to be a jest. The evening came down wet and dark when, looking out of window for her true lover, to her horror she saw a great cloud on the top of Bennachie and a causeway complete leading to the Mither Tap. She saw too the stranger coming for her and recognised him for what he was, the

Evil One. Flying desperately to Pittodrie Woods, she called upon heavenly powers and was turned into what is now called the Maiden Stone! There is in fact the remains of a stone causeway leading up to the Mither Tap, of uncertain antiquity, as there is evidence of the existence of an early fort on the Tap itself.

For a hill of under 1,700 feet in height, Bennachie has attracted surprising fame, both in legend and in verse. There is a stock of local ballads which sing of it and its guardian giant, Jock o' Bennachie, and, by contrary, of the Wee, Wee Man o' Bennachie. The most widely known of these ballads exists in versions which have been altered over the centuries and records the beauties of what is actually a modest and unassuming burn, the Gadie, in the parish of Garioch:

> *O! gin I war whar Gadie rins*
> *At the back o' Bennachie.*

The sterner ballads, however, tell of an event which had its importance for all Scotland: the battle of Harlaw, in 1411.

> *Frae Dunideir as I cam' throuch*
> *Doun by the hill of Banochie*
> *Allangst the lands of Garioch*
> *Grit pitie was to heir and se*

> *The noys and dulesum hermonie,*
> *That evir that dreiry day dud daw,*
> *Cryand the corynoch an hie,*
> *'Alas, alas, for the Harlaw.'*

Harlaw was one of the three or four great critical battles in Scottish history, for it virtually decided whether Celt or Saxon was to shape the course of the country's future. It took place a mile or so north of Inverurie. Of all elements most troublesome to the crown, Donald, Lord of the Isles, had invaded the north from his island stronghold and was sweeping all before him and threatening the destruction of Aberdeen. He had a force of probably 10,000 men, and he seemed to have it well within his power to break the grip of the Regent Albany in the country – the King, James I, being in captivity in England. The only hope lay in the Regent's nephew, the Earl of Mar. Mar was well known as far as England and Flanders as a doughty knight, but on this occasion his knightly accomplishments were perhaps of less account than the ferocious spirit which he had inherited from his father, the notorious Wolf of Badenoch. He gathered such men as he could, but they are said to have totalled only about 1,000. They made up for their meagre numbers in discipline and determination. The Highlanders' attack was devastating, but Mar knew their methods and stood his ground. The battle was one of the bloodiest ever fought in Scotland, and went on throughout the day, 24 July. Mar's losses were terrible. They included Sir Alexander Irvine of Drum, Leslie of Balquhan and his six sons, whose castle overlooked the battle, and the Provost of Aberdeen. But the losses of Donald were even more terrible, and when night fell he withdrew from the field. Mar was too greatly weakened to follow, but Albany himself pursued the advantage and forced Donald to make submission. Scotland breathed again, but as far south as the Lothians, as John Major records, boys played at Harlaw in their games.

Mention of Leslie of Balquhan and his sons raises the subject of the extraordinary resistance to the Reformers in the north-east, and especially in this corner of it, and of the survival of one or two fascinating relics of staunch Catholic sympathies. In Monymusk House itself there is a very beautiful Spanish wood-carving of the Virgin standing on the crescent moon, gesso-covered and daintily painted; but in the neighbouring barony of Fetternear the Leslies of Balquhan stuck to the old faith, so that this area between Bennachie and the Don is still strongly Catholic, served by the church of Our Lady of the Garioch. Fetternear House was a refuge for a wonderful collection of Catholic relics, most of which tragically were destroyed when the house burned down; but a few survived and were put on show at the British Association Meeting in Aberdeen in 1859, and were seen by the Prince Consort who came from Balmoral to address the delegates. One relic was given to the new church. It is a rare banner, later lent to the National Museum of Antiquities. This Fetternear Banner is not, as once believed, a war-guidon of the Leslies, but an ecclesiastical banner which, it is judged from the motifs embroidered on the linen, may have been made for the Fraternity of the Holy Blood whose altar

18. above *The Palace of Spynie. 19.* below *Pluscarden Priory*

was in the kirk of St Giles in Edinburgh. The Fraternity was of course dispersed at the Reformation, but the Rev. David McRoberts in a scholarly paper on the banner suggests it may have survived because it was not completed and handed over, so that somehow eventually it came into the keeping of the Leslies.

There are several great houses in this vicinity: Cluny Castle, Castle Fraser, and a little further north Fyvie Castle. Cluny is Victorian Scots Baronial, on the site of an older stronghold. Castle Fraser, a few miles to the east, is a magnificent pile, fifteenth-century completed early in the seventeenth by Andrew Fraser, later created Lord Fraser and confirmed as chief of the clan. 'Transformed' would be a more appropriate word than completed. The old tower was expanded to become a massive Z-plan castle with the help of one of the Bell family of masons whom we met with in the last chapter. His name, 'I. Bel.', possibly John Bell, appears on a stone on the north front together with the date 1617 and the letters MM with the outline of a heart and the letter F, which has been interpreted as signifying master-mason to Fraser, but it seems to me the MM might equally mean Muchal-in-Mar, which is the old name of the castle. This 'signature' occurs as an inset below what is surely the most superb piece of sculptured stonework on any of those castles: the royal arms above the Fraser arms, a commanding centrepiece rising up into the steeply-sloping roof and descending into the elaborately moulded, corbelled band which binds together the whole rambling building, tower, turrets and all. The clustered towers with their conical caps are even more than usually French. The French origin of the Frasers too is advertised by the repeated *fraises* motif, as the marriage link with the Douglases is by the heart, both occurring for example on the dormer window-heads. Castle Fraser is one of Scotland's greatest houses; and another is Fyvie, some distance to the north, close to the road to Turriff and to the River Ythan. Fyvie may be just outside the bounds of this book, but it forms such a climax in the story of the Scots Baronial style as seen in Deeside and Donside that it would be like lopping a limb to miss it out. The original castle, in which Edward I stayed during his invasion progress through the north, is long since gone, and the present

20. above *Leith Hall.* *21.* below *The 'Little Houses' from the Cathedral Gate, Dunkeld*

triple-towered pile is essentially a Renaissance building, a palace rather than a fortified place. The oldest part of it is the east tower, built in the fifteenth century by Sir Harry Preston when he was granted the lands of Fyvie on the battlefield of Otterburn. The Meldrum tower to the west is of the sixteenth century. Finally, Alexander Seton who, as Earl of Dunfermline, became Chancellor of Scotland, linked the two towers by building a central tower now given his name. He modified the existing buildings to make a symmetrical façade of the whole. The final touch is an enormous arched entrance for effect alone, for its bears no real relationship to the internal economy of the house. Fyvie is quite unlike the others of its kind, but it is an arresting sight as it is disclosed among the great trees and parklands by the Ythan. The most striking feature of the interior is the staircase, the finest stone staircase in any Scottish castle. It spirals up under a succession of shallow arches, undecorated except by a few small stone-carvings and some trophies of arms. It is not spectacular as the staircases of Blois or Chambord are spectacular, nor would it be easy to ride a horse up it, but there is something very French in its conception. I have doubts, however, about the theory that French masons built it, because the local school of masons was quite capable of doing it, and the stone-carvings are certainly Scottish. Mention of trophies of arms recalls that Fyvie is one of the few houses to possess a true claymore, the *claidheamh-mor* of the Gael. This great seventeenth-century two-hander with dipped quillons has a blade with the running-wolf mark of Solingen, for German blades were often used by Scottish swordsmiths. We cannot leave Fyvie without a reference to the stone trumpeter who tops a turret. It is in memory of Andrew Lammie, the Fyvie trumpeter and lover of Agnes Smith, daughter of the miller of Tifty a mile or two up the Ythan, and heroine of the old ballad 'Mill of Tifty's Annie'. The miller and his wife opposed the girl's marrying a trumpeter, and so ill-used her that she died of a broken heart. Her tombstone – a restored one – on which she is recorded as dying in 1673, is in Fyvie kirkyard.

It is not far from Fyvie to the source of the Ythan, the three springs called the Wells of Ythan. After the parklands of Fyvie, this is a bleak upland at the eastern end of Strathbogie, where the winter lingers into May, and there might seem to be small reason for going there were it not that this is the most northerly point to which it is known for certain the Roman legions penetrated. The place is Glenmailen, about a mile east of Wells of Ythan, but the marching-camp itself is on the right bank of the river. It should be said at once there is virtually nothing to see. How Colonel Shand, that redoubtable student of Roman remains during the later eighteenth century, managed to identify it is beyond praise. It is roughtly the shape of a parallelogram, covering 44 acres. The ramparts are almost obliterated by cultivation, but they were no doubt more obvious in Shand's day. For the mere impressionable layman, which is all I am in such matters, it is enough to stand on this windy height and wonder at the resolve of a Roman general to lead his men so far into hostile country. The general was in all likelihood Agricola. With the broad waters of the Moray Firth in the distance, the faint peaks of Sutherland beyond it, probably he went on further. He certainly had warships in the Firth in A.D.84. And we might go ourselves the few miles down the road to Forgue, the kirk of which happens to possess the oldest Communion cup used in the services of the Church of Scotland. The bowl of this lovely silver cup carries the punch of Henry Thomsone, an Edinburgh silversmith, and also that of James Cok as deacon of the craft, a combination which points to the date 1563 – for there were no date-letters in Scotland so early. An inscription shows the cup, with a companion piece, was presented to the church by James Crichton of Frendraught in 1633. Frendraught Castle, a mile or two to the south, was burned down in 1630, Viscount Melgum and the Laird of Rothiemay losing their lives. Frendraught was accused of murder and offered to stand trial, but an old servant was blamed and executed. It may be the cups were a thank-offering for his escape.

Just west of Forgue the road joins the A97, which in a few miles leads to Huntly, a pleasant, well-built market-town and capital of Strathbogie. Here the Bogie flows into the Deveron, which waters the fields and fertile meadows of the lower Strath. The most notable feature of the town is the ruinous castle to the north of it. Even as a ruin, roofless and with gaping, empty windows, it is impressive. Once a stronghold of the Comyns, in the fourteenth century it came into the hands of the Gordons, who rebuilt it. George Gordon, 4th Earl of Huntly, head of the powerful clan, opposed Mary Queen of Scots, and in 1562 was outlawed and defeated in a fight at Corrichie, and although he died a natural death his body was set up in a coffin before the parliament, which pronounced him traitor. His son supported Mary, but his son in turn plotted against James VI, who blew up the castle of Strathbogie as it was called then. When pardoned he set about rebuilding the castle, and as he had been educated in France it is not surprising he introduced French touches such as the row of oriels corbelled out high on the plain south front and once, as an old drawing shows us, dormered up into the roof as at Blois, where he is thought to have been governor. In 1599 he became the 1st Marquis. The restored castle in time fell into disrepair, and when Huntly Lodge was built close by the castle seems to have been used as a quarry for the stones.

Proceeding up Strath Bogie between hills which gradually grow higher, it is worth while turning off by the Kennethmont road to Leith Hall. This is not one of the grand houses, but it is a typical vernacular mansion, added to as needs required over the years. The original house, Peil Castle, was taken over over by the family of Leith of New Leslie, who added the north tower. There were further additions at intervals of a century and the final result is an enclosed courtyard. In 1789 the family name became Leith-Hay on the death of the Laird of Rannes. Andrew Hay, whose sister had married John Leith, this Andrew being the last of his line, and so things continued until 1945 when Mrs Leith-Hay of Rannes gave the Hall to the National Trust. Its contents afford a glimpse of the life of an honoured country family which, while not swaying affairs of state as the owners of places like Huntly Castle did, nevertheless sometimes were caught up by big events. The Hay side of the family at least was 'out' in the 'Forty-five. The writing case give to Andrew Hay by the Prince before Culloden is to be seen at the Hall, and a considerable collection of weapons of the period is also on view – indeed, many years ago I had the pleasant task of making a catalogue of them. Andrew was a giant of a man, 7 feet and more,

too dangerous to be included in the Act of Indemnity of 1747. The castle, in its way, is a gaunt memorial to a lost cause, the more poignant in that few probably stop to investigate it. Those who do will see the name John Gordon carved above the doorway, but it refers to the first of the line, the man who built the castle.

A short diversion may be made up Glenbuchat, by way of the Kirkton with its simple but pleasing little kirk, with its laird's loft, and on the west gable the date 1629. There seems to have been a Celtic church in the glen at one time, founded perhaps by a missionary named St Walloch, although no trace of it survives. It is a sheltered glen with a loamy soil, and there were signs of Iron-Age settlements, but they have disappeared. The road follows the Buchat Water up to Glenbuchat Lodge in the shadow of Geal Charn and the Ladder Hills, with peaks of 2,500 feet and more, which are the border between Aberdeenshire and Banffshire and outliers of the Cairngorms. Then it completes the circuit back to the Don and the main road which in a few miles more brings us to yet another remote castle, Corgarff, important enough to have been taken over by the Department of the Environment. Its strategic significance is obvious. It commands the meeting of three routes, to Donside, over the pass to Deeside and the south, and over the high moors to the north-west, so that it is not surprising it was rebuilt to serve the new military roads in the time of Wade. It is a tower-castle, and looks just the grim sentinel it was meant to be, deep in its enclave of high hills. It was, until not so many years ago, virtually the end of the road, for the route beyond climbs over the saddle between Beinn a Chruinnich and Carn Liath and rises to more than 2,000 feet. This is the notorious Lecht Road. When I first used to cross it by car it was not much more than a stony track, with hairpin bends in plenty and gradients of one in seven. We used to pause at the foot of the long climb and shut off the engine, to watch with interest the speck of a car in front labouring upwards and to listen if the day were quiet to the gear-changes. Not infrequently in those days the attempt failed and the distant, raucous sounds petered into silence but for the thin wail of a curlew. Over the horizon into which the Lecht vanishes lie Tomintoul and Strathspey.

149

CHAPTER SIX

Grantown and the Lower Spey

The Lecht road is the old military road over the hills to Inverness. It meets up with the Conglass Water coming down from Carn Liath. Away to the south is the deer forest of Glenavon through which the Avon, or A'an, tumbles from its loch under the precipices of Ben Macdhui and below Beinn a Bhuird and Ben A'an to be joined by the Builg Burn. The A'an brings down a big volume of water from those great heights, more in fact than any other river draining out of the Cairngorms, the Dee excepted, for neither Don nor Spey originate there. The forest of Glenavon is a dour, empty, rolling upland enhanced at times by glorious views of the high hills, those northern corries of which often carry their snow-cornices far into the summer. In the sixteenth and seventeenth centuries it was a wild country too, a land plagued by forays of reaving Farquharsons into Grant territory on Speyside, and the inevitable retaliations. MacGregors added to the troubles. After the 'Forty-five the garrison at Corgarff sent out its patrols and the Disarming Acts put reavers at a disadvantage, so that it became possible to use the grazings of Glenavon without the same risk of interference with the cattle. Then came the phase of town-planning which brought about several 'new towns', as we call them to-day, in the north: as it was said, 'even in the midst of the Grampian Mountains.' Among those proposed by the Duke of Gordon was 'Tamantoul', now Tomintoul. The problem of employment was to be served by a lint-mill and a spinning-school, and as there was freestone available for building, and limestone, and 'unexoustable Moss' (peat) for burning the lime, the future of the town seemed reasonable. But the Old Statistical Account (1794) records that the

150

thirty-seven families in the village had no manufacture to employ them; and the entry for 5 September 1860, in Queen Victoria's diary says: 'Tomintoul is the most tumble-down, poor-looking place I ever saw – a long street with three inns, miserable dirty-looking houses and people, and a sad look of wretchedness about it. Grant told me it was the dirtiest, poorest village in the whole of the Highlands.'

Someone in the eighteenth century had the idea of making Tomintoul into a spa by exploiting a mineral spring in the vicinity, but it was not until comparatively recent times that it began to attract summer visitors in any numbers, no doubt because the nearest railhead was Grantown. Its altitude of 1,160 feet – it is the highest village in the Highlands – may also not have recommended it to everyone, but there is good fishing in the Avon and the Conglass, and it has certain advantages as a centre for exploring, while it may yet develop as a skiing resort even if rather more exposed than its rivals in the Spey valley. Physically it has not, to my mind, the attractions of some of the other 'planned' villages of its period, but it has the spacious green which is typical. It tends to be dominated by the Roman Catholic church, and the old form of worship does survive here in an unusual proportion of families.

The B-class road leading north to Tomnavoulin might seem to promise little of interest scenically, but in a few miles it passes through a district famed right across the world. This is Glen Livet. Whisky is distilled in almost every part of Scotland, certainly throughout the Highlands and Islands, but Glen Livet would be accepted by most as the heartland of the industry and the first licensed distillery was here. The reason for Glen Livet's early ascendancy would, by most knowledgeable folk, be given as the water, combined perhaps with the pure, cold air of those northern slopes; but the main reason could be the inaccessability, for in past times it was as out-of-the-way as the forest of Avon where, as we have seen, authority was held in small awe. It was because of this that 'a popish seminary of learning' was able to survive here at a time when to be Catholic meant to be branded as a Jacobite sympathiser, and this in spite of alarmist warnings not only by the minister of Duthil but in pleas to the Synod of Moray – a seminary which, incidentally, eventually became the present-day Blair College near Aberdeen. The same remoteness served well the many stills which abounded in Glen Livet. It was in 1823 that private stills were made an offence. There had been long hostility in the Highlands to the notion of imposing Government duty on distilling, and more than one writer in our own time has described vividly how whisky had a price on its head as if it were a Jacobite fugitive, so that the hunting of it became a mark of tyranny in the eyes of Highlanders and was opposed even by ministers of the Kirk. At last the Duke of Gordon, who owned a major part of Glen Livet, took up the cause and said that if the Government would agree to a reasonable duty on the spirit he and other Highland landowners would do their best to promote the legal industry and to discourage private stills. What the Duke would have thought of modern duty-rates it would be interesting to know.

The distillery has a characteristic form and may be seen and recognised miles away. It is not exactly a beautiful feature in the landscape – although one distillery at least in Glen Livet has gone to extraordinary lengths to persuade us otherwise! – but time has added a certain respectability and it has become accepted like the hydro-electric dam. What may count in its favour is the knowledge that it is not an interloper, properly at home in Glasgow or Manchester, but something which has grown out of the virtues of these glens and mountains: the chill, crystal water, cool air scented by pine and heath, for drying the malt an uncontaminated peat as dug from the Faemussach Moss which for so long has served Glen Livet. And to these virtues may be added another in the case of this, the world's supreme malt-whisky region, extending from around Glen Livet westwards to the Great Glen: the barley-fields of the fertile Laigh of Moray. Sir Robert Bruce Lockhart and others have grown eloquent about these things, and most discerning and poetical of them all the late Neil Gunn. The literature of whisky is no doubt in some part fiction, but it is quite as persuasive as the beauties, obvious or subtle, of the countryside where the *Uisgebeatha,* the water of life, has been produced over such a long tale of centuries.

To push the bounds of the Highlands right to the Banffshire

sea-coast may seem absurd, but as one follows the Livet or other tributaries of the Spey northwards there is little sense of emerging from the hill-country or of leaving its place names or even its accents behind. Turning from Glen Livet into the Dufftown road, the eye is met by the deceptively gentle slopes of the shoulders of Ben Rinnes, whose peak is less than 250 feet short of the 3,000 mark. Glenfiddich Forest to the right of the road and Little Conval ahead also reach respectable heights, although the fine-grained rocks have weathered to no splintered peaks but only to seemingly endless, rolling, hog-backed hills. In the sheltered hollows towns have grown up. Emphasising once more the former remoteness of this region, like Tomintoul they are relatively new towns, planned by the landlords. Dufftown, appearing suddenly where Glen Rinnes widens, is among them. It dates only from the year of Waterloo, its founder the 4th Earl of Fife, James Duff, its plainly drawing-board plan a cross centred on the Town House. And as the water of the Fiddich is in all its properties close to Livet's, its source on Corryhabbie Hill distant only a mile or two from one of the sources of the Livet, Dufftown has become a town of famous distilleries. If it lacks historic buildings in itself, there are many in its vicinity. At Mortlach, to the south of the town, St Moluag founded a community of monks, and the abbot was made a bishop by Malcolm Canmore. The present church there is thirteenth-century, enlarged in the nineteenth but still impressive and in use, and containing a great deal of interest. There are tombstones of the fifteenth and sixteenth centuries, among them an effigy with the date 1549; but of more note perhaps is the evidence of Pictish occupation – a symbol-stone within the entrance and, in the churchyard, another bearing a somewhat crude cross which may be associated with the early monastic settlement. If one follows Glen Fiddich up for some miles the castle of Auchindoun appears high on a hilltop. It is founded within a series of ancient fortifications, sometimes erroneously described as Pictish but in fact prehistoric. The tradition is that it was built to resist the Danes in the eleventh century, but the ruins which we see are probably four centuries later and formed a Gordon stronghold. The massive tower has been associated with the name of Robert Cochran, the architect whom

James III so favoured that his indignant barons hanged him on Lauder Brig, and within the tower is a groin-vaulted chamber which Simpson describes as 'the noblest of Scottish festal halls.' The other Dufftown castle, north of the town, is Balvenie, which belonged to the Comyns and passed through the hands of several other families of note in the north, finally the Duffs. Within its walls was born Alexander Leslie, the Covenanting commander, one of the greatest soldiers of his time.

Four miles below Dufftown the Fiddich joins the Spey at Craigellachie. This is a small village, not to be confused with the Rock of the same name near Aviemore, bowered among pinewoods and a favourite resort for salmon fishers. The Spey is here probably attaining its fastest speed – and it is reputedly Scotland's fastest river – under the crag on its left bank. At this point the road crosses the river. A new bridge has been built to replace the one designed by Telford in 1815, a beautiful single-span arch it was, with battlemented towers on the Craigellachie side and, on the far side, the most disconcerting right-angle bend I have encountered anywhere, turning aside under a sheer rock-face. Just below is a black, sinister pool, evidently very deep. In the great flood of 1829 the water rose 15 feet at this point, but the bridge withstood it. The road goes by the Spey past Ben Algin to Rothes, a village which has almost as many distilleries as Dufftown, and thereafter through the Glen of Rothes to a sudden debouchment from the hills, the entire Laigh of Moray stretching across the north, and beyond that the Moray Firth, far beyond that again if the day be clear the sharp-edged high hills of Sutherland. After many miles of narrow glens the sky seems enormous. Five miles away are the spires of Elgin.

In spite of its being an arm's length from the hill-clountry, Elgin is as much a gateway to the central massif of the Highlands as Aberdeen is, or even Perth. The Laigh of Moray, despite its fertile farmlands and its wide horizons, is ethnically and historically bound up with its mountainous hinterland because it is a small plain with its back to the sea and all but one of its main communications lie up through the glens and over the moors to the south.

154

Like Edinburgh, Elgin is a town of two periods. There are not two distinct towns, as in Edinburgh, for the periods mingle: vernacular, mainly of the seventeenth century, with Georgian work of the eighteenth and nineteenth. The stone is the same light-coloured, locally-quarried freestone, whatever the period, and the result is a charming marriage. The layout is very simple: a long, gently-curving street, the High Street, linking the hill where the old castle stood with the cathedral in the low-lying meadows by the bank of the Lossie. The High Street has its modern shop-fronts, but quite a number of the original frontages survive. In 1773 Dr Samuel Johnson still found it possible to walk 'for a considerable length under a cloister, or portico', and he remarks that this arcaded walk was probably continuous at one time, but that new buildings have intruded on it. One one of the best arcaded houses left is Braco's Banking House, at No. 7 High Street. The arcades have been filled in with shop-windows, but the form of the house is unspoilt, and there is a characteristic courtyard with white-washed houses behind. The date on one of the dormer pediments is 1694, and it was just after this date that the banker, William Duff of Dipple and Braco, came to it. The house of Dean of Guild Ogilvie at No. 50 is another good example of burgh architecture at the end of the seventeenth century. The wynds and closes which break the street frontage, if they have not the grandeur of the Edinburgh closes, are in some cases just as picturesque. Elgin too had its town mansions. The finest of them was Thunderton House, just off the High Street. Charles Edward stayed at Thunderton House before the battle of Culloden and his hostess, Mrs Anderson, kept the sheets in which he slept and 25 years afterwards was buried in them.

The town's focal point is the cathedral. The third largest in Scotland, Professor Hannah called it 'the most satisfactory church that ever rose on Scottish soil'. Elgin became the seat of the bishops of Moray in 1224, and the cathedral was completed before the end of that century. It was an enlargement of the existing Kirk of the Holy Trinity, and the building of such an elaborate structure so far noth seems to have been due to the enthusiasm of Bishop Andrew de Moray, who at one time had been at Lincoln, and the munificent patronage of the king, Alexander II, and probably also to the support of the wealthy Norman lords who had been brought in to replace the rebellious element in Moray under Malcolm IV. The result is a lovely building which, although small in scale by English, to say nothing of Continental standards, nevertheless was choice of its kind and worthy of the title which it won, the Lantern of Moray. Only about a century after its completion, the Wolf of Badenoch partially burned it down in revenge for a rebuke from the Bishop over the ill-treatment of his wife. Famous for its lofty belfries, its wealth of decoration and its jewels and relics, as he said, the Bishop was broken-hearted, but slowly over the next century it was restored. Another threat to it came in 1402, from Alexander, Lord of the Isles; but, in the face of a threat of excommunication, Alexander held his hand and part of his penance is said to have been the erection of the Little Cross at the junction of North College Street and the High Street, although it should be said that only the copestone of the existing cross could be original. At the time of the Reformation the cathedral was again a noble building, with a twin-towered west front and a lofty central tower, the whole surrounded by the group of manses known as the College of Chanonry which still survives in the building wrongly designated the Bishop's Palace and the Deanery, now called the College. The reformers did not destroy the cathedral, but the neglect which followed 1560 had the same effect in the long run. In 1567 the Privy Council ordered the lead to be stripped from the roof to be sold to pay the soldiers' wages, although the cargo was lost at sea on its way to the Low Countries. There is probably some case for the disbelief of Dr Johnson, who felt the order was intended primarily as a popular one. Weather, of course, did the rest. At last, in 1809, steps were taken to remedy the situation. A custodian was appointed, a poor, ne'er-do-well shoemaker called John Shanks. To his everlasting credit, his responsibility caused his reform and he set about clearing the site with his own hands, moving 3,000 barrow-loads of rubble and collecting the fragments of stone-carving and laying bare the ground plan, so that the tablet to his memory bears an epitaph by Lord Cockburn:

> *Whoso reverences the Cathedral will*
> *respect the memory of this man.*

Now the ruins and precincts have had some of their dignity restored so that the empty shell, seen across the tree-studded lawns of the Cooper Park, does lend the air of a cathedral city. It is to be hoped that current proposals for a bye-pass road to relieve traffic congestion do nothing to injure this.

The Museum of the Elgin Society at No. 1 High Street provides an interesting commentary on the town and district. Even the one-time trend for Anglo-Indian familes to retire here to this mild and fertile spot seem to be reflected in an unexpected collection of oriental material. But perhaps the most significant objects are the Pictish relics in the entrance hall, the stone-carvings of bulls from nearby Burghead. We have followed traces of the Picts right up through the Highland borderlands, but the bulls of Burghead are unique. None of this people's animal sculptures show better their ability to combine with marvellous economy of line the qualities of realism, brilliant symbolism and a faultless decorative sense. There were at one time, it is said, about 30 such bulls, but it is impossible to know whether one man or a school of carvers was responsible. What is probably the finest now lies in the Edward VII gallery of the British Museum, and there are two more in the National Museum of Antiquities in Ediburgh. The Elgin Museum is left with only two originals. My own view is that where conditions are suitable, as they are here, people should have to make the pilgrimage to the locality where such things were made to see the finest examples. But for all we know there may be more hidden somewhere at Burghead itself, since some may have gone into the rubble packing the south quay of the little fishing port.

The north road out of Elgin to Lossiemouth strikes through a new housing estate, then runs in long, straight stretches over a countryside not very inviting from a distance, yet because of its immense horizons oddly compelling. The land drops towards a wide basin actually below sea-level, and not so far back in time an inlet of the sea. Wave action formed a reef of sand and shingle, and the resulting land-locked basin became the Loch of Spynie, and this four centuries ago apparently was a beautiful piece of water with a wooded margin. An island in the loch carried Spynie Palace, where the bishops of Moray lived, and the island has become a knoll where the ruins of the palace survive. As we have seen in the fate of Elgin Cathedral, there were many marauders in the hills with an eye upon the orchards and granaries and other riches of the Laigh, so that the 'Lords of Spynie' had to be prepared to use their temporal as well as their spiritual might. They made their palace into a castle. From here they presided over a considerable empire, as may be judged by Bishop David de Moravia's founding of the Scots College in Paris in 1313. The last of his line is reputed to have been in league with the Evil One. It is an eerie place, and if one walks down that road into the haze of a summer gloaming with a dull red glow marking the meeting-place of sea and sky it is not hard to call up the vision of a great flight of witches reputed to have been seen on All-Hallows Eve making for Spynie, and to imagine the speck of welcoming light in the window of the bishop's room, even if the witches were a skein of homing geese.

There is a similar legend associated with Gordonstoun, a few miles to the north-west. Out of Elgin, the road diverges from the road just described and descends past Duffus castle to the village of the same name where the road breaks west to Burghead and east into the Gordonstoun drive. Most of those who know of Gordonstoun as a famous but quite new public school are unaware its buildings have a long history. Gordonstoun House, now the central feature of the school, is a composite structure with seventeenth-century wings. Seen from the great south lawn with its herbaceous borders, it is a gracious and rather lovely house. The original portions no doubt date from the day when the Marquis of Huntly was the owner, although there was an earlier fortification. It passed into the possession of the Sir Robert Gordon who gave it its name, and those Gordons had much need of dungeons and secret passages. They had the right of life and death – of 'pit and gallows', in the old phrase – over their servants and tenants. Sir Robert, the first baronet, was in favour with James VI and his successor, which made it easier for him to plunder the countryside. The most interesting of the Gordons, however, is specially associated with an odd building known as the Round Square. Originally, this was a series of stables and the like built on a circular plan around a cobbled courtyard. The story goes that the

22. above *Castle Cawdor.* 23. below *The Square, Grantown-on-Spey*

Sir Robert who built it made it circular so that the Devil could never get him in a corner, and there is no doubt that in his day this man had a sinister reputation and was known as the Wizard of Gordonstoun. It was said that, when studying in Italy, he had made a pact with his sinister master, and that he had pawned his shadow to escape his clutches, so that even in brightest sun he cast no shadow although his horse and his belongings retained theirs. He kept a furnace perpetually burning and in the heart of it brought to birth a salamander that would do whatever he bade it. When at last the Devil came to claim his own, Sir Robert is reputed to have tricked him into giving him more time by declaring that the clock was fast, so he could fly for sanctuary to the kirkyard of Birnie. The minister of Duffus fled with him, but fell behind. He was overtaken by a terrible man on a black horse with two black hounds at its heels, and lied he had not seen Sir Robert. But a distant yell of agony came back to him, and presently the dreadful rider reappeared with the corpse of Sir Robert across his saddle-bow. Next dawn the minister was found dead with the marks of the hounds' teeth in his throat. Yet in reality this same Sir Robert was, as might be suspected, a man of learning, living where he was not understood and shutting himself away with his books. He invented, among other things, a sea-pump so efficient that it was used in the Navy. It brought him into correspondence with Samuel Pepys, and another of his correspondents was Sir Robert Boyle, the great natural philosopher and enunciator of that Boyle's Law which no doubt has its place in the Gordonstoun curriculum to-day. He must approve of the use the school has made of his Round Square for the one-time stables have been turned into dormitories and common-rooms and what must be one of the most pleasing school libraries in the kingdom. One of the wisest parts of the policy laid down by the late Kurt Hahn and his successors has been their determination to keep green local traditions and to sink the school's roots deep in the soil of Moray.

If Gordonstoun survives through a change of use, Pluscarden Priory has had its ancient way of life resurrected. It lies beside the Lochty or Black Burn, a tributary of the Lossie, in a sheltered dell once called the Vale of St Andrew. The priory for centuries was

24. Fort George from the air

roofless and a semi-ruin, and only in 1948 was it bestowed on the Benedictines of Prinknash Abbey in Gloucestershire, who sent some of their number to see what could be done. There are only a few of these men, but they have worked methodically and hard after consulting with an architect, the late Ian Lindsay, responsible for so much fine restoration work in Scotland, and much has been achieved. They have among them masons and a wood-carver and even an artist in stained glass, and they have gradually brought back amenities to the abbey church, at the same time keeping themselves by cultivating the fields and building up a stock of bees. The white-habited monks moving about their tasks seem to transport us back seven hundred years. The scene in those times is described graphically and in detail in Peter F. Anson's book, *A Monastery in Moray,* in which he points out that the monks would have conversed in French. They exerted an excellent influence on the turbulent district, not only spiritually but also through their reputation for scholarship, and in the fifteenth century they compiled a history of Scotland called *The Red Book of Pluscarden.* The burgeoning fields and the well-stocked salmon and trout streams, however, became a source of temptation, for the priory grew rich and began to use its riches in the pursuit of power. A Benedictine called John de Boys was sent from Dunfermline in 1470 to re-impose discipline for, as Professor Hannah puts it, 'the light of their quire had not been reflected in the lives of the Valliscaulian monks!' The first priority in the reconstruction naturally is the big church itself, the style of which is late First Pointed, but the beautiful Lady Chapel is in use as the monastic choir.

The main road west out of Elgin soon becomes level and runs in long, straight stretches, with few features except a stand of pines at intervals. But in the far distance appears a hill with woods and a monument atop of it, marking the town of Forres. It is an agreeable town, with a rather surprising feature as one enters from the east: one of the most beautiful cricket-grounds in the kingdom, set in the shadow of the hill; but the most important monument in the place is tucked away on the left of the road to Findhorn, which breaks back from the A96 just at the town boundary on the east. It is a sandstone monolith 23 feet high called Seuno's Stone. Joseph

Anderson regarded it as the most remarkable monument in Britain. It is baffling to archaeologists. The wheel cross on its south side might seem to link it with the Pictish stones which we have met with so often in the north-east; but none of them has anything to compare with the elaborate battle-scene on Sueno's Stone, depicting chained captives and decapitated bodies. This persuades Douglas Simpson to dissociate it from 'the peppery but kindly Celts' – forgetting, perhaps, the gruesome practices recorded by those same Celts in their sculptures in south Gaul. But it does seem to be a memorial to a great victory: captives and corpses are the usual symbols of a mighty king's prowess in ancient Egyptian or Assyrian art. Perhaps the most credible association is with the tale of the invasion of Moray by Sigurd the Powerful, Earl of Orkney, in A.D. 900, when he was opposed by Maelbrigd, mormaer of the province, a grim-looking warrior with a single protuding tooth. He challenged Sigurd to a fight with 40 picked horsemen on either side, but the treacherous Sigurd put two men on each horse. I should have thought this to be a questionable advantage, but the Northmen slew the men of Moray, cutting off their heads and hanging them from their saddle-bows – incidentally, another old Celtic custom! But Sigurd, the ghastly head of Maelbrigd at his horse's flank, scratched his leg on that protruding tooth and, within three days, he died. Some believe the headless bodies identify this as the monument over Sigurd's grave. The Sueno whose name is now given to the stone was the son of Harald, King of Denmark, whose men routed the Scots under Malcolm II at Forres in 1008.

A granite boulder on the other side of the road, but further on, recalls that practice of the black arts associated with Spynie and Gordonstoun, but which had real enough and grim sequels hereabouts. Forres's association with witches is an ancient one and so widely known that it brought Shakespeare to use it in *Macbeth*, and Boswell recalls how Johnson got out of the carriage on their way across the 'blasted heath' in order to declaim the appropriate lines. There is little purpose in trying to identify a heath in a tale which Shakespeare read about in Holinshed, who lifted it from Boece, who wrote his chronicle far from the heath anyway; but this wayside boulder brings a piece of grim fact into the welter of superstitious tales. The very King Duncan whom Shakespeare used as the first victim in his bloody account is said to have been smitten with a puzzling disease after staying in Forres Castle, and three local witches were siezed and condemned for sorcery. Their fate was not unlike the fate of Regulus. They were jammed in barrels with spikes inside and pushed off the top of Cluny Hill. It can hardly be that this is one of the three great stones erected to mark the place where the barrels stopped, for Cluny Hill is at some distance, but it is known as the Witches' Stone. These unhappy witch-hunts persisted here until the seventeenth century, and a number of poor women were strangled and burned as late as the reign of Charles II. It brings one uncomfortably near the dark age represented in *Macbeth*. As one of the clan descended from Macbeth's father, the first mormaer of Moray, I might perhaps say 'misrepresented', for historically speaking Macbeth was something of an heroic figure, in spite of his slaying of Duncan; and Shakespeare, in the interest of his drama, as the late Sir James Fergusson claimed in *The Man Behind Macbeth*, even 'suppressed altogether Holinshed's statements that Macbeth governed with justice and made "commendable lawes".'

From Forres, we turn back towards the hills by the Grantown road, which approaches the Findhorn river and skirts the Altyre Woods. Across the river is Darnaway Forest, and in its midst Darnaway Castle, chief seat of the earls of Moray. It dates only from 1810, a formal block with odd little concessions to the national style in the shape of tiny turrets at intervals along the roof-edge, but in the rear is a relic of the old structure, a splendid fifteenth-century hall known as the Hall of Randolph. Sir Thomas Randolph was the first Earl of Moray, so created by Robert the Bruce. He it was who scaled the nearly sheer face of the rock of Edinburgh Castle and surprised the English garrison, and later in that year of 1314 helped Bruce at Bannockburn. And among many tokens and records of the family's history preserved at Darnaway there is, in Randolph's Hall, that gruesome protrait of the 'Bonnie Earl' after his murder at Donibristle when, with his last breath, he is said to have told his chief assassin, Huntly, 'You have spoilt a better face than your own.' Above Darnaway the Findhorn comes down through a gorge which it has cut in the sandstone, driving left and right in a series of dramatic scenes enhanced by hanging pinewoods up to a rocky feature on the Relugas policies known as Randolph's Leap. On a summer morning, the woods filled with birdsong, it is idyllic; but on the path down to the Leap, high above the river, is a stone which they tell you marks the height of the flood of 1829. The Findhorn is typical of these short Highland rivers with an enormous catchment area. Sir Thomas Dick Lauder left an enthralling account of the 1829 disaster, seen from Relugas itself, where he was tenant. He tells how a black cloud gathered, filling the sky with darkness and the countryside with a bronze twilight; how a tempest arose that tore limbs from the trees; how the cloud broke, away to the south on the Monadhliaths, where the Findhorn rises; and how a wall of water came down the little valley carrying rocks before it and made a noise like thunder and the cannonade of battle combined. At Relugas the gardener caught a salmon with his umbrella 50 feet above what should have been the river. A wooded hill 100 feet high is said to have been swept away. And when this mass of water emerged on to the lower ground, carrying the new three-arched Findhorn Bridge with it, the whole plain of Moray seemed to be submerged under a muddy flood with the sails of fishing vessels from the coast moving over it in search of survivors, and, in one account, 'in danger of foundering from trees'.

Before Relugas, the main road leaves the Findhorn and follows the Divie for a time, then comes upon the great expanse of the Dava Moor. It is commonly described as lonely and barren, and on a grey day so it is, but I have a special feeling for it because, as a boy, I spent many summer gloamings trying to cast a fly on the streams that wind through it under the patient tuition of a forester on the Castle Grant policies. With the low sun glinting on black pools in the peat hags, it is a haunting place; and it is equally haunting on a June afternoon to lie on a tussock in the middle of this tawny waste and watch a hawk circling against the blue and hear the intermittent, far-off coo-ee of curlews. And lying there one thinks, rather incredulously, of how even into this remote spot six centuries ago came that ubiquitous monarch, Edward I, with a great army of knights, men-at-arms and bowmen. He came on 28 September

1303. His objective was the castle on the islet in Lochindorb, invisible at first from the main road but accessible by the side-road near Dava station. The castle was a Comyn stronghold, but John Comyn abandoned it in the face of such strength. Edward occupied it for ten days. He is thought to have strengthened its defences, and he certainly held court here and issued writs and indulged in the chase after deer and boar not only on the moor but in the forests which in those days blanketed the higher ground around the loch. in 1371 the castle and the lordship of Badenoch were conferred by Robert II upon Alexander Stewart, his fourth son, and he, through his terrible deeds to become known as the Wolf of Badenoch, is the man with whom Lochindorb is chiefly associated. So difficult to reduce was it that in 1445 James II, anticipating the part it might play in resistance to him, ordered the Thane of Cawdor to raze and destroy it.

South of Dava the road climbs to the railway, which strikes through a cutting and pine plantations and makes its way down into Speyside, which is the country of the Grants. On the left are the policies of Castle Grant. Unhappily, the castle is now part-derelict. Forty years ago it was still occupied, in later summer at least, by American millionaires who rented its extensive grouse-moors; but it suffered the fate of so many of those Highland castles used by troops during the war, and the last time I saw it there were broken windows and flapping blinds. Not that it was one of the handsomer castles: Queen Victoria likened it to a factory. But it was an historic house, filled with interesting relics. A few years ago they included some at least of its unique collection of Highland guns, a rare and beautiful type of firearm with a Moorish look about it, the greater part of the two dozen or so surviving examples of which were housed under this roof. One of these guns appears in a portrait which hung, when I was last there on a wall of the castle. The subject is a ferocious-looking clansman, and the picture is called 'The Champion'. As lately as the beginning of the nineteenth century great state was still maintained at Castle Grant, and a contemporary description is a fascinating record of what was probably even then the usual practice in a chief's household. It is drawn from that wonderful source-book, the

Memoirs of a Highland Lady, written by Mrs Grant of Rothiemurchus.

> Generally about 50 people sat down to dinner there in the great hall ... There was not exactly a 'below the salt' division so marked on the table, but the company at the lower end was of a very different description from those at the top, and treated accordingly with whisky-punch instead of wine. Sir James Grant was glad to see his table filled, and scrupulous to pay fit attention to every individual present; but, in spite of much cordiality, it was all somewhat in the king style, the chief condescending to the clan, above the best of whom he considered himself extremely.

The persisting feudalism of such a gathering underlines the hierarchy of the clan system. It should also be noted that the traditional drink of a Highland gentleman was wine, the wine imported from Bordeaux in such quantities, not the whisky which the caterans brewed in their stills among the heather.

A mile or two down the road is Grantown-on-Spey. It is yet another, and perhaps the best example, of those 'created' towns. The initiator here was Sir Ludovic Grant of Grant, who invited merchants and others to take feus in the year 1765. What had been moorland in a few years became a well-planned township with a spacious square and solid, pale grey buildings of local granite. Other Grants contributed to the amenities of the town, among them Lady Grant of Monymusk, part of a bequest from whom, on the advice of a Dr Gregory Grant, went to an orphan hospital for children from local parishes. Originally, wool and linen manufactures were intended to provide employment, and the second did prosper for a few decades. The moor around became fields and birch and pine plantations, which gave a sharp, sweet tang to the keen air, and when the railway came in 1863 Grantown became potentially attractive to visitors, for it is a good centre for a wide area of interest. Hotels sprang up, one or two of them quite large, but until the last war at least it remained a pleasantly tweedy sort of resort, with fishing-tackle to be bought and at least one shop which dispensed guns and cartridges, with which I recall my forester friend making me acquainted in aid of certain nocturnal expeditions in the surrounding forests. The clientele of Grantown seems to ,have changed. Jeans and open-necked shirts are more numerous than tweeds in the square, and of course there is the universal plague of cars; but I think the invasion of commercial tourism is not quite so obvious as in one or two other places further up the Spey, and the ski schools do provide a winter season.

The country south and west of Grantown will be covered by the two succeeding chapters. East of the town the river winds in a series of great loops skirting the Hills of Cromdale, a name itself said to derive from the Gaelic for a 'crooked plain' because of those loops. It is hardly in any sense a plain, but has been easy to cultivate even in early times if the occurrence of various stones of Pictish origin, now much neglected, is anything to go by. It is now good upland farming country, with considerable tracts of forest. The hills are a rolling eight-mile ridge, brown with heather, like all the hills hereabouts deceptive as to height, for several of their summits are above 2,000 feet. Congash, at the Grantown end of the hills, shows most evidence of early habitation, but the village from which the hills take their name has limestone deposits in the vicinity, a comparatively rare blessing for Highland farmers which seems to have been fully exploited. The old Cromdale village has disappeared, although it must have been a prosperous place, with an annual fair, a court-house, a jail, even a hanging-hill. Its fame, however, has been kept alive by various ballads:

> *I met a man wi' tartan trews,*
> *I spiered at him what was the news,*
> *Quoth he, 'The Highland army rues*
> *That e'er they came to Cromdale.*

The reference is to the battle fought in 1690 on the slopes above the village, the Haughs of Cromdale. In point of numbers it was more a skirmish than a battle, but it ended the resistance to King William in the Highlands. Three hundred men of Clan Grant aided the Government force, but lost Hamish, their piper as he played a coronach for the dead.

A few miles on, the Avon plunges down through fine hanging woods to join the Spey. The road swings up the gorge of the Avon to meet the Tomintoul road and back again at a sharp angle towards the Spey, by the policies of what is perhaps the only real masterpiece on Speyside of the baronial style so well represented on Dee and Don. This is the castle of Ballindalloch, another seat of the Grants. The date 1546 is carved over a fireplace in the oldest part of the house, and Patrick Grant added the corbelled cap-house in 1602. The wings are eighteenth-century. In 1829 a flood from the Avon threatened the building, rising several feet in the ground-floor and leaving only the tops of the fruit trees in the garden visible, but the castle survived and twenty years later was re-modelled with a care and tact not always shown in this period. An area beside the drive known as the Castle Stripe is said to be the site originally chosen, but legend has it that when building began each day's work was undone by supernatural agency in the shape of a great night wind from Ben Rinnes, and when the Laird himself kept watch he too was blown into the gorge, like the stones of his house, but above the storm he heard a fiendish voice telling him to build in the cow-haugh – which is where the present castle stands.

CHAPTER SEVEN

Badenoch and the Upper Spey

Several chapters ago, we left the Great North Road where the Bruar Water comes down to join the Garry. We take up the journey north again here and begin the long haul up Glen Garry. Haul is perhaps a word no longer applicable. It used to mean two green locomotives with hissing outside cylinders harnessed like two great horses in tandem to overcome the gradient. Now a big, dark diesel does it in its stride, and the new road is so smoothly graded that cars no longer have to change gear, and the Garry itself no longer plunges from one black pool to the next since the hydro-electric schemes have robbed it of its water, while road-contractors' vast spills of excavated material make the glen look like an industrial waste-ground. Not that those huge hills were ever beautiful, for they are rather featureless masses, their flanks mottled and patchworked by the heather-burning, but they had a gloomy grandeur, and the cloud-ceiling as often as not obscured their crests to lend this approach to the great central watershed an air of drama which always kept my face, as a small boy, glued to the carriage window. But if the sleek new road takes one past the summit without one's knowing it, there is still something about the Drumochter Pass. The signs by the railway announce 1,484 feet, which is the highest altitude reached by any railway line in this country, and as the ominous bulk of the Sow of Atholl gives place to the equally ominous shape of the Boar of Badenoch, an eye kept on the watercourses will detect that they are now running north instead of south. A few miles on, just as Dalwhinnie comes into view, a long glen opens to the left and light can be seen glinting on the waters of Loch Ericht.

The loch leads away south into a remote, wild country. It is about 16 miles long and is fairly narrow, and it is overhung by some magnificent hills which comprise Ben Alder Forest. Ben Alder itself is at the far end of the loch from Dalwhinnie, and to climb it or any of the group involves much long and difficult walking, some of it through bog presenting even harder going than is usually to be looked for in Highland glens. These are not hills for a ramble on a summer afternoon. Like some of the Cairngorms, Ben Alder offers a huge area of summit plateau of a sub-Arctic character, rising to its peak at 3,757 feet. But it is visited by climbers rarely by comparison with the more accessible mountains. Although the waters of the loch have never been known to freeze, this is a country with a long and inhospitable winter and likely to deter winter-sports enthusiasts for a long time to come. It deterred troops as dogged and determined as Cromwell's Ironsides, who could not tackle the clans in these fastnesses. It also offered secure shelter to Charles Edward after Culloden, and the maps mark a spot as Prince Charles' Cave on the south shoulder of Ben Alder. 'That dismal mountain of Ben Alder', as Stevenson describes it in *Kidnapped*. The 'cave' is known as 'Cluny's Cage', and it is described as being made of stakes and interwoven branches with a living tree as the centre-beam of the roof, so that it is clear Stevenson got his particulars from Robert Forbes' *The Lyon in Mourning,* the account of the 'Forty-five which appeared within a generation or so of the event. There is nothing now but boulders, and no sign that trees ever grew here. Forbes may have manipulated his facts, as he probably never visited this place; but Cluny Macpherson himself after Culloden had hiding-places enough in Badenoch to conceal him for nine years, kept secret by his clan and tenantry.

At Dalwhinnie, back on the Great North Road, we are in Glen Truim, but the landscape before us opens wide and the hills roll back. Often, too, the heavy clouds which have filled Drumochter may be seen to disperse ahead as the long stretch of Strathspey appears. The main road follows the Truim down to the Spey. Another road forks left to Lagganbridge, where it meets the main route westwards by Loch Laggan and Glen Spean, and the Spey comes down here from the slopes of Carn Leac and the

Corrieyairack Forest. As we approach the Spey a reminder looms
ahead that this is still the country of Cluny Macpherson, though his
descendants are dispersed far and wide. It is a great rock-mass,
tree-girt: Craig Dhubh, the Black Rock. Here, high on a crag, is the
cave which was the chief lodging of Cluny during the nine years
when the redcoats were after him, and it is fitting that the slogan,
the war-cry, of his clan is *'Craig Dhubh Chloin Chatain!'*, which is to
say 'The Black Rock of Clan Chattan!' Tragically, when at last the
Chief escaped to France he died within a year and is buried at
Boulogne, far from his clan burial-ground, where his wife lies. And
the home which he is believed to have watched burning from his
hiding-place on the rock four miles down the river, at the hands of
Cumberland's troops, has been replaced by a nineteenth-century
Cluny Castle, for the clan lands were restored to the family in 1784;
but the Cluny Macpherson has departed from his castle, and the
Jacobite relics which it still contained a hundred years ago – the
silver-mounted shield of Charles Edward with its Gorgon's-head
boss, the charmed ancestral belt, the pistols and swords and dirks –
have gone also. Some, however, were bought by the clan during the
last war. They are housed in the clan museum in Newtonmore, and
they include the Green Blanket of Clan Chattan and the Black
Chanter, which is like the Fairy Flag of Dunvegan said to be a gift
of the Little People.

The next village down the Spey is Kingussie, projected by the
Duke of Gordon late in the eighteenth century on the site of a priory
founded by George, Earl of Huntly, in the fifteenth. The Gaelic
from which the name is derived means the end or head of the fir
wood. The slopes are still well wooded which shield it from the
north, the slopes of A'Chailleach and Carn an Fhreiceadain, spurs
of the Monadhliath, the Grey Hills, which face the Monadhruadh,
the Red Hills, the true name for the Cairngorms on the other side of
the Strath. The spinning and woollen manufacture which were
intended to support the village never prospered, but it has grown
into a township and the virtual capital of Badenoch largely because
of its situation athwart the Great North Road, with good access to a
variety of amenities. Always a summer resort, it now participates in
the general tourist development of Speyside. Its chief cultural asset

comes from the fact that Dr I. F. Grant chose it as the final home of her great collection of Highland byegones and relics which she housed first on Iona, then at Laggan. She gave it the name Am Fasgadh, the Shelter. Her enthusiasm and her vast knowledge brought her collection to life for all those fortunate enough to meet her, but in time she felt she had to hand over her creation to a trust supported by the four older Scottish universities. Am Fasgadh then became better known as the Highland Folk Musuem. Its first curator under the new order, 'Taffy' Davidson, himself a collector, had a formidable fund of information ranging from Highland weapons to lore about the ancient pearl-fisheries. Two old houses on Spey Street formed the original museum, but much has been added, including reconstructed dwellings such as a Lewis black house and a thatched water-mill, and the main displays cover all aspects of old Highland life from period rooms to an exhaustive range of agricultural implements. This apart, there is not much of past history to be found in Kingussie. Across the Spey, however, is a monument which can be seen for miles around, the ruins of Ruthven Barracks on their great mound. They lie beside what might be called the Inshriach road, which parallels the A9 on the opposite side of the river and is infinitely more attractive than the main route, not least because the long-distance lorries and articulated vehicles do not take this way. There were castles on this mound from an early period, one of them belonging to the Comyns. In the seventeenth century Ruthven was visited by John Taylor, the Thames waterman who is known as the Water Poet, who made the visit in the company of the Earl of Mar and was decked out by the Earl in full Highland dress. This castle probably was of traditional form, but Claverhouse destroyed it in 1689; and when in 1719 a decision was made to lodge a Government garrison here the ruins were cleared completely, incidentally disclosing timbers in the foundations which seemed to confirm that the mount on which the castle stood was artificial. The barracks were built on very different lines from the original structure. They formed a stronghold, however, loopholed for muskets, and were capable of a stout defence; but they fell before a Jacobite attack under Gordon of Glenbucket shortly before Culloden, and a force of two or three thousand waited here after that decisive defeat in the hope that Charles Edward would continue guerilla action from remote hide-outs among the hills. Ruthven is the most notable of the Government strongholds of its time, and its decay has been arrested by the Ancient Monuments section of the Department of the Environment.

There was a village of Ruthven hereabouts in the eighteenth century. In it was born in 1736 one James Macpherson who, after studying at Aberdeen and Edinburgh universities, returned as village schoolmaster. At the age of 24 he published what were represented as fragments of ancient Gaelic poetry, and a year later he claimed to have discovered an epic 'composed by Ossian, the son of Fingal'. Its authenticity was challenged, notably by Dr Johnson It is generally accepted now that this and later works of 'Ossian' Macpherson are in fact inventions of his own in the main; but it also recognised that, more importantly, they are works of genius very much in the vein of the ancient epics. Unlike some men of genius, he received much acclaim in his own time too, and his admirers varied from Goethe to Napoleon. He held some curious posts – secretary to General Johnstone in Florida, London agent to the Nabob of Arcot – but finally became a member of Parliament, for Camelford. He was a man of wealth. In 1790 he bought the lands of a former robber-chief, Macintosh of Borlum, just a mile or two beyond Kingussie, and built a house to a design of Robert Adam which he called Belleville, a curious choice of name now altered to Balavil, the original name of the property. The house, on high ground to the left of the road at the village of Lynchat, survives, but the poet is buried in Westminster Abbey.

Kincraig village is not strung out along the main road as Newtonmore and Kingussie are, but is pleasantly grouped on lower ground and overlooks Loch Insh, through which the Spey flows. It is one of the old Celtic church sites, and the present kirk on the mound called Tom Eunan, which is to say hill of Adamnan, is a reconstruction of a much more ancient building. It is a beautiful little church, but its real treasure is the bronze bell of St Eunan. Those old Celtic hand-bells are simple, beaten out of sheet bronze, later sometimes preserved in 'shrines', as with two examples in the

National Museum of Antiquities and the world-famous shrine of St Patrick's Bell in the National Museum of Ireland, but it is a special privilege to see one housed on the site where it may have been in use 1,400 years before. The story goes that this bell was carried off to the south, but in the Drumochter Pass gave tongue to its name and, by one account, flew back itself to the church by Loch Insh. Kincraig also is the gateway to Glen Feshie. This glen is the only easy passage through the mountain mass walling Speyside in on the south, and there was even talk at one time of driving a highway through it to Deeside, a desecration which it is to be hoped the opening up of Speyside will do nothing to encourage. The lower part of the glen, around Feshiebridge, is beautiful. Further up, in Glenfeshie Forest, it is desolate and rather wet going, but it curls round behind the southern massif of the Cairngorms and gives easy access to a whole group of Munros – Meall Durbhag, Mullach Clach a Blair, and the great mass which straddles the Inverness-shire–Aberdeenshire border, Monadh Mor and Beinn Bhrotain. The last two offer an easy slope from this side; they present a darker and more frowning aspect to Glen Dee beyond.

We return to the Great North Road. Above Kincraig begins Alvie parish, and with it a stretch of pleasant, open country with thousands of silver birches and everywhere a faint, subtle, aromatic perfume of mingled birch and heath. The Strath is opening out, and the horizon is vast and rimmed with hills. It is a country which has endeared itself to many people, none more so than the nearly legendary Jane, Duchess of Gordon, who spent her summers and autumns in Kinrara, to the right of the road, its policies running down to the Spey. There she busied herself all day – Mrs Grant of Laggan describes her as rising at five to supervise her workmen – and entertained far into the night her many distinguished visitors. Indeed, there is a gay dance which is called after Kinrara. Her best-known exploit is the raising of the Gordon Highlanders, and she is said to have persuaded the more hesitant recruits with a full kiss on the lips. She is buried at Kinrara:

> *A sigh shall breathe for noble JANE,*
> *Laid low beneath Kinrara's willow.*

She died in 1812. Later the estate passed out of the hands of the

Duke of Gordon, whose monument is on a hill nearby, and it has had several owners since. An etching hanging on my wall recalls one of them: it was a present to me from Lord Bilsland of Kinrara to record an association of many years ago. And he is buried in a little kirk which is well worth a visit, a little white kirk on a promontory in Loch Alvie, which the road skirts just after the entrance to Kinrara. This is another very old church in origin, but it has been rebuilt several times, most recently by Sir Basil Spence, who has a very sensitive way with what is old. One memorial in the kirkyard lies over the grave of 150 skeletons found about a century ago under the church, and quite possibly the casualties of a forgotten battle on the spot.

Two miles beyond Alvie the road makes a wide bend and passes between newly-engineered embankments which prepare our eyes somewhat for the sight of Aviemore. It was never the most attractive village on Speyside. Its chief feature in my boyhood memory was the railway station which presided over the junction between the Inverness line and the branch to Grantown and Forres. Now Aviemore has become the Highland centre of the tourist industry, and millions have been poured into it, creating hotels and other facilities of a kind wholly foreign to the Highland landscape. There are two ways to look it it. There are those who argue it brings to 'this beautiful environment the sort of person who would never discover it for himself or, if he did discover it, would never put up with the lack of such amenities as cinemas, swimming-pools, skating-rinks and bingo halls to which he is accustomed. Or there are the outrageously conservative snobs like myself who maintain that if a visitor is not prepared to take the country as he finds it he has no business to be there at all. It must be conceded that this kind of thing has brought an all-the-year-round season, with business almost as brisk in winter as in summer, not only because of the numerous ski-schools but also because the place has become a conference-centre for delegations often so irrelevant to the environment as to be funny; but one wonders just how much of the consequent prosperity really finds its way into the pockets of the native community and how much of it goes straight to shareholders in distant cities in the south. I am, of course, prejudiced. I would not trade the home-baked scones and shortbread which used to be available in the tiny teashop as you entered the village from the south for all the sophisticated restaurants now on offer. I propose therefore to avert my eyes and to hasten under the railway-bridge towards Rothiemurchus and the hills, for those last still look as they always looked, if the approach is not quite as it was.

The great doorway to the Cairngorms stands wide open for all who come to Aviemore to see. It is the deep gash in their skyline, the Lairig Ghru, the high pass which leads across to Braemar. Often there are clouds in its throat, bringing darkness into it. The track up to it is a long one, four miles and more from Aviemore by way of Coylumbridge, and it passes through Rothiemurchus which, with neighbouring Glenmore Forest, forms the largest surviving area of the ancient Caledonian Forest. This does not of course mean an area of dense timber. There are big, old pines and young pines distributed over a heathery ground-cover, with some birches and a scattering of juniper. But the most beautiful spot in Rothiemurchus is at Loch an Eilean, reached by a forest road branching off between Aviemore and Coylumbridge. It is so accessible to the popular resorts around, and has been so praised by so many, that the silence imposed by the great trees crowding in upon the water's edge is now often interrupted, but footfalls are softened by the deep carpet of pine-needles. The name means Loch of the Island, and it is the tiny island which is the centre of interest, because the castle on it has been the stronghold of many owners over the centuries, first among them reputedly the Wolf of Badenoch, later the Shaws and Grants. MacCulloch, that ubiquitous chronicler of Highland beauty spots, has an eloquent description of it which records that 'the eagle has built his eyrie in the walls' and he claims to have counted the sticks in his nest; but clearly the bird he means is the osprey, of which this was the last nesting-place in the Highlands until it returned to the Loch Garten area in recent times.

Retracing the road to Coylumbridge, there are two tracks direct to the high hills, one of them to the Lairig, the other through Glen Einich. I recall it was the second track we took when I first ventured into the Cairngorms more than forty years back, the objective being

177

Braeriach. Like all those granite hills, it is not especially impressive from far off, but after one passes the lower bothy in this glen – a tragic place, because a party of winter climbers about the time I am talking of just failed to see they were close to it in a blizzard, and died – the real scale and nature of the hill are seen. We climbed between the Coire Ruadh and the Coire an Lochan, the lochan far below, dirty snow still veining its precipices. The summit of Braeriach is an extraordinary place, four miles of tableland above 4,000 feet. In winter the climate is arctic, but in summer it is an exhilarating place, carpeted with mosses and lichens which would be fodder to reindeer but not much else. A few steps from the cairn, the great Garbh Coire opens, with precipices on three sides, old snow in their shadows, the screes of Cairn Toul plunging steeply to the source of the Dee in its spring-fed pools. We climbed down slowly into the chill dimness of this enormous amphitheatre and made our way into the Lairig Ghru, which is at its most spectacular at this point. The precipices of the Corrie darken the west. To the south, beyond Cairn Toul, is the Devil's Point. To the east frowns the face of Beinn Macdhui. Northwards, the Lairig mounts to its bleak, shattered summit. The Pools of Dee lurk among the debris of old avalanches, water which is ice-cold and of an eerie green translucency. And from somewhere among the rocks comes that strange and somewhat disturbing sound, the grunting of cock ptarmigan.

The Lairig bisects the central Cairngorms. The great tops to the east of it – Beinn Macdhui and Cairngorm itself – are normally approached from Loch Morlich in Glenmore Forest, an area which has been 'developed' in recent years, commercially and with subsidies from the Highlands and Islands Board, and a new road served by car-parks and a snack-bar make it possible even for the faint-hearted to go very high with the minimum of effort. I must qualify the effects of my obvious resurgence of prejudice about 'development' by recording that much is to be said on the credit side, first because the Glenmore Lodge project has instructed innumerable young people in the basic knowledge of climbing and hill-walking, and the dangers involved, and second because the organisation of the ski-slopes here has made it possible for thousands to acquire skills which they might never have dared to seek in the Alps. And if Cairngorm has been rendered rather too accessible, Macdhui, at 4,286 feet the highest of the range, is still aloof beyond the deep chasm which in its depths holds Loch Avon. Like Braeriach across the Lairig, Cairngorm and Macdhui together form a vast plateau, and although the summit of the first is a little more obvious than Macdhui's there are no dramatic peaks to give point to one's sense of achievement. The reward lies rather in the distant views, and from Macdhui can be seen on a clear day virtually the entire procession of the Highland peaks, with the possible exception of the Cuillin of Skye. The nearer heights across the Lairig seem tremendous, Cairn Toul especially. On a fine day the walk between those two great hills is a magnificent experience, with very little rough going to preoccupy the thoughts. If there is bright sun on the top, by contrast the plunging views of Loch Avon far below are into a well of darkness. Down there is Clach Dion, the Shelter Stone, a huge fragment of the precipice which has crashed and is poised on other boulders and can give some kind of cover to anyone caught in this inhospitable spot by storm or mist. In high summer it could provide not merely bed but some sort of breakfast, because there are blaeberries in plenty around it and cloudberries too, that larger and much rarer fruit which one associates rather with Norwegian mountains. And right up under the shoulder of Macdhui, at a height of over 3,000 feet, is the phenomenon of Loch Etchachan, in which it is possible to find trout, although they must be stout fish which find their way from the headwaters of the Dee up Glen Derry into this lofty corrie. It is tempting to spend many hours investigating those high, sub-arctic plateaux, but no matter how blue the sky and how hot the sun it is wise to keep a wary eye on the peaks in all directions, for clouds and mist can creep up swiftly while one is lying face down beside the ice-cold spring which, surprisingly, wells up not far from Macdhui's summit. Those heights are no place for wandering in mist, as there are too many sudden drops. And, of course, there is the spectre. An entire book has been written about *Fear Liath Mor*, the Great Grey Man, whose relentless tread has been heard by climbers somewhere behind them, even by experienced alpinists. Sounds can be much altered by those mists on the high hills, and although I have never heard or seen the Grey Man of Macdhui, I have more than once felt my hair rise when alone on another hill I watched a rock-pinnacle loom out of the trailing skirts of a cloud just as though it, and not the cloud, were coming to meet me.

The forests of Glenmore and Abernethy three centuries ago must have lapped the lower slopes of Cairngorm and its northern outliers like a dark green sea. Exploitation of such natural assets began long before the twentieth century. After the 'Fifteen forfeited estates began to come into the market, and apart from that many landlords acquired a taste for the ways of the south and wanted ready cash to pay for luxuries. In 1728 the York Buildings Company bought part of the forest of Abernethy for £7,000, and half-a-century later the same kind of thing was going on, for in 1783 a Hull merchant bought the whole of Glenmore forest from the Duke of Gordon. Some of the timber was used to make charcoal to smelt iron ore, an industry which decimated Scottish woodlands; but the splendid old trees of Glenmore – one is reputed to have furnished planks of six-foot width – were used to start a shipbuilding yard at the mouth of the Spey, and in 22 years 47 ships were launched, one of 1,050 tons. For long the trees were floated down the Spey in rafts. The devastation wrought by those exploiters has been lessened by natural decay and growth, but in a little book published in Aberdeen only just over a century ago the wreck of the ancient forest is described as 'a melancholy but a terrific spectacle', with a few lofty trees standing like gigantic skeletons. 'It is', says the writer, 'one wide image of death'. The authorities were perhaps not sorry to see such cover destroyed for Glenmore and Rothiemurchus hid many fugitives such as John Roy Stuart, the Gaelic poet and rebel colonel, who lurked there after Culloden until he managed to get away to France, only to die in the French King's service.

It is in the Abernethy forest that the osprey has again found a refuge to enable it to nest and breed. At one time it was common in the Highlands, and possibly regarded as a sort of eagle, because Mrs Grant of Rothiemurchus in her girlhood, like MacCulloch whom I have quoted, wrote of the Loch-an-Eilan birds as eaglets and of their nest as an eyrie. The osprey properly is a fish-eating hawk. The Abernethy sanctuary is preserved only by constant vigilance, and has been raided, but it has become a tourist attraction and is indicated by direction-signs which make it easy to find. This forest is also a haunt of the capercaillie, which lives on the buds of the Scots pine, young shoots and such fruits as blaeberry, blackberry and any other berries it can find, but it is wary and not so often casually encountered. To come upon a big cock bird suddenly is an experience startling to both parties, for it is as large as an eagle and its take-off and rush through the lower branches of a thick plantation is like a small whirlwind. The thick ground cover and relative dryness of those Speyside forests, and their warm clearings filled with resinous scents, attract many sorts of moth, and ant-hills are numerous among the pine needles. Inevitably, the popularity of the area must pose an increasing threat to it. Boat-of-Garten – 'boat' signifies an old ferry across the Spey – used to be a very small resort, in summer mainly frequented by hill-walkers, but it has now grown out of recognition. Before the war the Nethybridge road across the river from the village was the boundary of as untrodden a piece of forest land as one could wish for, with Loch Garten the jewel in the midst of this great setting, but it is now very much a tourist attraction. Beyond the loch, on the other hand, lies the main area of the forest and the Nethy river which comes steep, and short and liable to sudden spates, from its source at the back of Cairngorm. This is one of the routes to the Lairig an Laoigh, the Calves' Pass, named presumably from its use by the drovers, which crosses the shoulder of the Bynack Mor and so on to Glen Avon and Deeside – an easier but much longer way than the Lairig Ghru. But to return to the Nethy, east of where it passes through the forest are the Braes of Abernethy, a high, lonely country still and, lying on the north slopes of the Cairngorms, inhospitable in winter. In 1804 a party of soldiers walking home on Christmas leave from the south encountered a blizzard here and one only, a sergeant, survived, carrying a dying comrade. It was also a country of rough justice, and the old Statistical Account records several stories of summary hangings here, especially by two men of the name of Grant, one known as Bailie More and the other as Bailie Roy, the second of whom varied his practices between hanging thieves and parboiling their heads and drowning them in sacks. A third, called Bailie Bain, so outraged the people that they turned the tables on him and drowned him in the Spey.

Nethybridge, which straddles the Nethy just before that river joins the Spey, by contrast is a sheltered and attractive spot which used to be a resort for older and less energetic visitors than those drawn to villages nearer the high hills, although that may have changed. Its history is unremarkable, but just north of the village on the Grantown road is the ruin of an old keep of the Comyns, the Wolf of Badenoch's kin, known as Castle Roy. Simpson speculates it may have been the home of Augustin, Lord of Inverallan, in the thirteenth century. More definite associations attach to a place on the other side of the Spey, just above where the Nethy comes in. This is Tullochgorm or Tullochgorum, which has given its name to one of the best-known reel-tunes which, from the district, have come to be known as strathspeys. The tune was composed by a well-known eighteenth-century fiddler, Hamish Dallasach, but the song put to it by the Rev. John Skinner was held by Burns to be the best of all Scotch songs. Skinner made it up at a hostess's request to end a political squabble, and to find rhymes for Tullochgorum he makes witty play with words like Whiggamorum and quorum.

A short distance down river the Dulnain joins the Spey. It is a good salmon river, and so Dulnain Bridge has always been a favourite village for anglers. But if there is no great weight of history or tradition upon Dulnain Bridge there is more to be said about the next small village, Duthil, four miles further west. Its old name was Gleann-a-chearthernich, the Glen of Heroes. Perhaps Freebooters is a better translation than Heroes, for the annals of the place read like tales of the Wild West. There is, for example, the cattle-raid of the Laird of Achaluachrach, whose victim picked a posse and went after him, coming up with the Laird and his party in the night and bringing them down with their arrows. Little John Macandrew pinned Achaluachrach himself to the post he leaned against, but he had no liking for it when a delighted companion shouted 'God and victory be with you, John Macandrew, who dwell in Dalnahaitnich!', for he knew he would be a marked man. In due course avengers arrived but, not recognising him, they asked where John Macandrew lived. He took them to his house and told his wife, doubtless with a wink, that the men wanted to see his master when he came home. She gave them a meal. Meanwhile John went out and climbed a tree where he kept his bow and arrows, and when he shouted he saw his master approaching the men ran from the house and were picked off easily. This parish also seems to have been a haunt of wolves, and it is said that as late as around 1700 the forest of Duthil was burned down to destroy the animals; but on the other hand the account which claims that many surviving wolf-traps prove the case seems doubtful as it was written a century and a half after the menace had been dealt with. Similar statements are made about the Slochd area to the west. It was certainly wild and lonely enough, and there were deer in plenty and other game for the beasts to prey upon, and it seems to be accepted that it was in Mackintosh country just beyond the Slochd that the last wolf in Scotland was destroyed in 1743.

The Dulnain road joins the Great North Road at Carrbridge on the edge of the high moors stretching away from the Monadhliath to Strath Dearn. Carrbridge has not suffered from the big-scale investment which has changed Aviemore out of recognition, but has become almost as much an all-the-year-round resort, with ski-schools – some with Swiss or Austrian names – asserting their presence. Here the scale of development is still in keeping with the environment, and the one major enterprise, the visitor centre called Landmark, is discreetly and appropriately situated among the pines. This is something of a pioneer venture which with considerable success attempts to describe and interpret the background of history, geology and natural history in an entertaining way rather on lines which I have myself recommended for local museums in another book. The structure maker extensive and tasteful use of timber, an admirable thing in a countryside where the sounds and resinous scents of sawmills are still present. Unfortunately the main street of the village is also the A9, and the traffic of tankers, articulated vehicles and other primitive impedimenta of an urban society is unceasing day and night, while the growing grip of new heavy industries in the north will only add to this. A bye-pass is essential. Personally I would prefer a tunnel, where the noise and stench could be buried deep, like sewers . . . .

The main feature of the village, from which it takes its name, is the old Bridge of Carr across the Dulnain. It is a high-arched structure built about 1719 as part of Wade's system of military roads, and although the great flood of 1829 reduced it to a fragile skeleton which looks as if one push would bring it down it clings to its dark, gneissian base-rocks as if it were part of them. The Dulnain has its source in the Monadhliath among a group of peaks which rise to around 3,000 feet. It can be followed for a considerable distance by a road and track through pleasant scenery of moor and birch and fir, and at Sluggan there is another high-arch bridge over the Dulnain. It replaces a Wade bridge, for the military road came this way, not by the present route. Despite the occupation forces the Carrbridge country, like all Duthil parish, continued lawless until far into the eighteenth century, and there are many stories of cattle-reaving and reprisals, the most bloodthirsty perhaps associated with Tom-nan-Cean, the Hill of Heads, the heads being those of Muggach-mor and his six sons, and the murderer himself was hanged with a rope of birch twigs seven years later at the spot. From Carrbridge the Great North Road climbs with the railway high over the moors. From those moors the whole of Speyside stretches off southwards, the green, cultivated areas merging into the blue and purple of the Cairngorms, in season capped with white. Then the road mounts to the summit of the Slochd Mor, a narrow defile through an outlying spur of the Monadhliath. This is the watershed. Beyond it the streams flow north to the Moray Firth.

CHAPTER EIGHT

Inverness and Glen Albyn

Inverness is the natural metropolis of the entire Highland region. It is peripheral to the central area which we are dealing with in this book, but if we include the northern and western Highlands and the islands of the Hebrides beyond, then only Inverness commands easy access in every direction. This can be seen at a glance by anyone approaching by the Great North Road as it descends from the heights of Drummossie Muir, disclosing ahead the smoke and the steeples and chimneys down there in an amphitheatre of hills. Beyond the town the sea glints, the shallow arm of the Beauly Firth. Beyond that is the Black Isle, and beyond that again the massif of Ben Wyvis; unseen to the south-west is the Great Glen, Glen Albyn, the straight route to the Atlantic seaboard. In days when all journeys had to be undertaken by what is now called 'surface travel', which means virtually throughout the course of history, Inverness straddled the way of all comings and goings of importance in the north from the arrival of Columban Christianity in the sixth century to the final passing of the Divine Right of Kings in the person of Charles Edward Stuart in the eighteenth.

For a centre of such predestined importance, the town may well disappoint expectations, visually at least. There is hardly an old building left in it, and the steel-and-concrete accretions of the last ten years or so have been erected, as it seems to me, with a singular absence of any sense of what is proper in what, after all, is the Highland capital. To dwell briefly on one instance only, the reconstruction of buildings in Bridge Street, east of the new bridge over the Ness, not only ignores the opportunity offered by a challenging site, but contrives to detract from the one dominating building in the town, the nineteenth-century red sandstone castle on its hill, which houses the county offices. The castle may have no great virtue as a building, but at least it shows awareness of the duty to do something about amenity. For the rest, the streets of the town are narrow and rather tortuous. For a stranger attempting to go directly through the place on his way to the north or west, it is hard to say which is the more frustrating: to try to follow the directions for bye-passing the town-centre, or to go boldly through it, bottle-neck though it be. Commercialisation, concrete and the internal-combustion engine have wrought havoc with a town which in my boyhood still had a Highland quality about it, a faint tang of peat-smoke such as one can scent at times in Dublin, a country tweediness in the streets and shop-windows, and in the same windows a goodly complement of guns and fishing-tackle. To say this no doubt is evidence of nostalgic hysteria in the view of economists and developers, who will point to the increase in population and employment, and to the presence of the Highlands and Islands Board headquarters and the Crofters' Commission, to say nothing of the North of Scotland Milk-Marketing Board and a growing number of factories and industrial depots of one sort or another. This, they will claim, is the way to real prosperity and importance. Some of those things are appropriate enough: the Highlands Board, for example, and the Crofters' Commission. But in the long-term interest of the Highland capital there should first have been a study in depth of what such a capital could and should be, and this long before a sod was turned. Not that the blame belongs with Inverness alone. If, for example, as I have stated in the Introduction, there was need to add to the number of the four ancient Scottish universities, one of them should have been sited in the Highland capital, where it might have become a main centre for Celtic studies and therefore meaningful. That there is no institution of higher learning north of a line drawn from Aberdeen through Stirling to Glasgow is quite incomprehensible.

Even a lengthy stay in Inverness would not produce much material evidence for its being a historic town, but there are a few pointers. We know that about the year A.D. 565 the High King of the Picts, Brude MacMaelchon, was converted to Christianity by

Columba, and we are told it happened at the king's palace on the banks of the Ness. For palace no doubt one should read fort. There is the remains of a fort on Creag Phadrick a mile or two west of the river's mouth. The hill on which the castle now stands is perhaps a more probable site, although yet another hill, Torrean, has claims and in 1808 produced a massive silver chain – in Wales such chains were worn by certain kings instead of crowns. There are a few fragments of Pictish sculptured stones of local origin in the town's museum on the Castlehill, among them a superbly-outlined wolf from Ardross, dating perhaps to a century after Brude's time. There was certainly a medieval castle where the present castle stands. Edward I held it on two occasions. At other times it was in the hands of Robert the Bruce, Edward III and the Lords of the Isles. Here too Mary Queen of Scots made merry in 1562 after riding all the way from Edinburgh, and said she longed to be a man and 'to lye all night in the fields'. By 1651 the castle must have been ruinous, because in that year Cromwell's army set about building a fort in what is now the dock area. It is usually called the citadel, but more than one later writer, Boswell among them, refer to it as Oliver's fort. There is only one building left which existed when Cromwell's garrison was here. This is Abertarff House in Church Street, a sixteenth-century structure which takes its name from the estate of Archibald Fraser of Lovat who, however, acquired it only in 1801. It is now the property of the National Trust for Scotland which has restored it beautifully and has leased it to An Comunn Gaidhealach, the Gaelic Society, and has become a sort of information centre for things Highland, an appropriate function. The only other good example of vernacular architecture in the town is the nearby Dunbar Hospital, built just after the Restoration by Provost Alexander Dunbar as an almshouse.

Even the eighteenth century is represented by few remains other than the High Church, yet this is a period about which there is no lack of written evidence, from Boswell, Pennant, the egregious Captain Burt, and even General (then Major) Wolfe of Quebec fame himself. The only one of them who leaves a picture of a place in any way attractive and prosperous is Pennant. By his day it had perhaps got over the aftermath of the 'Forty-five. Its sympathies were strongly Jacobite, for several of the neighbouring chiefs had their town residences there, and it is not surprising there were routs and balls and much gaiety when Charles Edward and his army came there in February 1746, the prince residing in the house of Lady Drummuir, a house subsequently occupied by the 'Butcher' Cumberland, on a site which is now No. 43 Church Street. The early years of the Government occupation were in contrast to the brief weeks when the Prince lay in the town. The letters of Wolfe are as disgruntled as the letters of Burt had been a decade earlier. Burt disliked nearly everything about the Highlands, whether the hideousness of the hills, 'especially when the heather is in bloom', or the kilt, which he calls the Quelt and considers to be indecent. Wolfe also had no time for Highlanders and grouses about the weather and his rheumatism as though he had been 55 instead of a mere 25, and he disliked the tones of the 'Erse' tongue – although Defoe long years before had remarked on the purity of the English spoken in Inverness – yet he was ready enough to enjoy the company of 'female rebels' and on one occasion danced with the daughter of Macdonald of Keppoch himself, who had died at Culloden.

In its natural features Inverness has all the advantages any town could wish for. Among them is the river. Although only six miles long from its emergence from Loch Ness to its entry to the Beauly Firth, it is shallow and wide and has at one point a group of long, narrow islands in it which are well wooded and connected with a parkland and gardens on the bank by means of small bridges. On a summer night when the lamps are lit and there is a twilit sky the scene is more like one of the Rhine resorts such as Boppard than a Highland town, and if there are no illuminated river steamers moored to the banks the air 'sweetly recommends itself unto our gentle senses' – how did Shakespeare discover this? – while in winter there is a traffic of magnificent salmon here on their way to the deep waters of Loch Ness. The hilly features around may not be capped by any Rhineland castles, but they are pleasantly wooded in contrast to the bare, blue distant mountains. The nearest of them is Tomnahurich, which is famous as a cemetery but also as the best viewpoint in the town, which Pennant appreciated.

188

The approach to Inverness by the Great North Road has in itself a certain strange quality of revelation. After the Slochd summit the country tilts northwards and the sky seems to stretch and one senses something new beyond the horizon. Here it is rather empty country. To the right there is Moy and its loch, seat of the Mackintosh of Mackintosh, chief of the great confederation known as Clan Chattan, then the road slants down into the valley of the Nairn and climbs out of it again past the prominent little kirk of Daviot, burial place of the Mackintoshes, which now has to face a stone-quarry the white dust of which settles everywhere, part of the price to be paid to make it easier for the road-tankers and articulated vehicles whose contents should have been transported by rail anyway. Once over the top at Daviot interesting name-signs begin to appear, pointing eastwards along minor roads just as one begins to see that marvellous panorama of the Ross-shire and Sutherland hills far off to the north. One of those roads goes by way of Strath Nairn, skirting Beinn Buidhe Mhor, and bears the sign 'Cawdor'. In this Macbeth country, it is an evocative name, and neither the village of the name nor the castle close to it will prove disappointing. The castle, to my mind, is the choicest of all Scotland's medieval castles, the more so since its ancient features have not only been preserved but lovingly kept alive by a certain degree of tactful adaptation to the needs and ways of to-day. Like so many Scottish castles, it has grown over the years. The original stronghold, Thane William's tower, was built in the mid-fifteenth century on a rocky outcrop overhanging a burn flowing down to the Nairn and is protected in front by a dry moat crossed by a drawbridge the suspending poles of which project from embrasures in the wall behind. A small courtyard divides the entrance from the tower-keep itself. The other buildings which ramble delightfully around the tower were added by Sir Hugh Campbell in Restoration times. The lovely tones of the stonework are enhanced by creepers and by flecks of colour where small plants or mosses seem to have lodged in crevices, and the setting of great trees and, to the south, of a truly choice walled garden with many rare plants in it complete the picture and make one wish that more of our ancient places had been cared for like this. The interior redoubles the wish. I have stressed in another book that the only satisfactory way to keep our heritage of such castles and mansions not only preserved but alive is to make it possible somehow for them to be lived in, implying of course that those who live in them must love them. Cawdor has been fortunate in this. The fifth Earl, for example, combined with his learning – he was an antiquarian of high standing – a warm enthusiasm which was infectious whether he was pointing out the landscape from the windly battlements of the tower or explaining the significance of the dead hawthorn tree in the dungeon far below. The legend relating to the tree is that Thane William had a dream directing him to put the coffer of treasure he had amassed to build a tower upon the back of an ass and to erect the tower wherever the ass stopped, and that the animal did so at the third of three hawthorn trees growing from a rock. The tower was built around it. In strange contrast, when I saw it there was lying nearby the handsome nameplate of a locomotive with the device: *Thane of Cawdor*! It is difficult to choose between other features of the interior and impossible here even to touch upon them all, but mention must be made of Lady Cawdor's bedroom, immediately above the great hall. Its stone walls are completely covered by a set of tapestries illustrating the story of Noah commissioned at Oudenarde by Sir Hugh and Lady Campbell for this very room about 1685, and in the charter-room of the castle are the papers recording the transaction and the charges for transporting the hangings from Flanders to the mouth of the Findhorn River. The magnificent bed with its wine-red velvet curtains also dates from Sir Hugh's day, and is one of the finest Restoration pieces of its kind in Scotland.

After this road to Cawdor, the next sign or two on the Great North Road points the way to Culloden. The suburbs of Inverness already have an outlier or two not far from the battlefield, but it is shielded on the north by the Forestry Commission's forest of Culloden, and on the south there are open fields stretching to the Nairn. The only structure surviving from 1746 is the little thatched house known as Old Leanach cottage. The battle monument in a clearing of the trees, with a bush growing on its top – they say no broom will grow on the graves on the other side of the road –

is an appropriately austere memorial, but the information centre of the National Trust for Scotland, which now owns the battlefield, is prominent enough, although in itself excellently designed. The centre contains a small theatre where there are regular audio-visual performances describing Prince Charles Edward's ill-fated progress from his landing in Moydart to his ultimate departure in a French frigate after his months as a fugitive following his defeat at Culloden. In Old Leanach cottage are a number of relics and some plans of the battle. But nothing is so evocative as to stand alone outside, there to think on the tragedy of those forty fateful minutes, especially if – as happened to me not long ago – it is early on a misty April morning, and one realises suddenly it is as near as need be to the 16th. The opposing armies were drawn up facing one another diagonally across the route now taken by the road, the Jacobites with their backs to the west. The course of the battle is too well known to need repeating; there is no better concise guide to it than the Trust's own, by Colonel Cameron Taylor. It is the old story of impetuous Highland bravery against a trained professional army, but the terrain was ill-chosen from the Highlanders' point of view, and they were unrested and had had little food. In a situation like Killiecrankie things might have been different, but with no obstacle to Cumberland's dragoons and no protection from his artillery the outcome was a foregone conclusion – or nearly so. And the Prince, insisting on taking command himself, was no commander. It seems that the tale of the notorious sulk of the Macdonalds because they were not given pride of place on the right of the line is ill founded, and that Keppoch's cry that the children of his tribe had forsaken him is misrepresented. Colonel Stewart suggests the legend may have been put about by Whig historians to sow dissension among the clans, and they were well capable of doing so. It would be a mild measure by comparison with others taken by the Hanoverians in the aftermath of the battle. Even the well-known incident of Wolfe's refusing to pistol a wounded Jacobite when commanded by Cumberland – or it may have been Hawley – to do so shows up, in the light of the evidence of Wolfe's own correspondence, as not so much an act of clemency as the refusal of an officer and a gentleman to lower himself to the role of

191

executioner, and that is a literal enough interpretation of his own words. The appalling behaviour of Cumberland and his troops in the hours and weeks following their victory – and one must recall that not all those troops by any means were Englishmen – is a commentary on the state of society in the eighteenth century which might well modify our horror about what happened in France in 1789. Was the guillotine worse than the burning of the wounded Highlanders in the barn marked by the scattered stones beside Old Leanach cottage, or the casual bayoneting of the dying seen by the surgeon counting the dead in the evening of the battle? And there is good evidence that the Jacobites, however ferocious the Highland onset, were much more civilised in their behaviour to defeated enemies. But the most remarkable outcome of Culloden is that this ground over which it was fought has become more hallowed than any other battlefield in Britain. Scots from Lowland parts which in the 'Forty-five hated and feared what Charles Edward stood for are now more moved by this little area of Drummossie Muir than they are by the sight of Bannockburn, and many an Englishman or woman whose ancestors may have jeered at the executions at Carlisle or York, or at the head of rebels on the spikes at Temple Bar feel the same sense of desolation here as they listen to the peewits dipping an crying across the fields. As to the Highlanders, they have long memories. Not many perhaps attend the annual service, mainly conducted in the Gaelic, held on the morning of the Saturday nearest to the 16th at the memorial cairn, but the Mackintosh and other kilted figures will be there; and at its end I have seen a woman so carried away that she fell upon the grave of her clan and embraced it, and then drank with her cupped hands from the Well of the Dead.

A few yards from the battlefield there is a cross-roads, one route from which leads to the Clava stones, which are near a farm beside the right bank of the River Nairn. The 'stones' are in a long, wooded meadow by the roadside, and consist of three chambered cairns, each surrounded by a circle of monoliths. The chambers are roughly twelve paces in diameter, and access in two cases is by a passageway. All were of course roofed over at one time, presumably by false vaulting, that is by the stone courses gradually converging until they came together. The cairns would be used for the entombment of men of high rank, those with passages probably for more than one burial. The precise significance of the stone circles around the cairns is uncertain, but those to the south-west are the loftiest, a feature which has been noted in other places, and which would seem to suggest some sort of relationship with the position of the sun which must have had a ritual significance. There are also the remains of paved pathways, possibly processional ways. On the evidence of the passage-grave tradition, Douglas Simpson has suggested the cairns may be of the Bronze Age rather than Neolithic, but as they date from 1500 B.C. or earlier in this northern region the latter attribution must seem to be the more likely. They are among the best preserved relics of their time in this country, and are under the care of the Ancient Monuments division of the Department of the Environment.

Under the same supervision is another monument a few miles to the north, and 12 miles west of Inverness. It is Fort George, at the tip of the Ardersier peninsula which projects towards the Black Isle and divides the Inverness Firth from the much wider waters of the Moray Firth. Fort George is one of the places which everybody knows about, but which only a relatively small number of people ever visit, and let it be said emphatically that it is well worth making the diversion from the A96, the Inverness-Nairn road, because in spite of the fact that it never came under attack it is one of the most remarkable artillery fortresses to be found anywhere. The forts existing at the time of the 'Forty-five proved to be rather ineffective, and those in the Great Glen were reduced by the Jacobites without great difficulty. Fort George would have been a very different matter. The best knowledge and skill of its time went into the building of it, and its location, with sea on two sides and open country on the third with no high ground near enough to command the defences made it fairly impregnable to any but a powerful and well-equipped army, certainly to any force which the shattered and disarmed clans were likely to be able to recruit. To the lay eye there is something awesome in the approach to this fortress. One crosses the gently-sloping glacis, commanded by outer fortifications, deeply angled, behind them Prince Edward's

Ravelin with a deep ditch before it, and a much broader ditch behind it. This is crossed by a wooden bridge, originally fitted with a drawbridge. Behind this great ditch rises the curtain wall linking the Prince of Wales' and the Duke of Cumberland's bastions, in the centre a fine classical gateway surmounted by the sculptured arms of George II. Once past the gateway one looks down upon a wide lawn, formerly the parade ground, at the far side of which are the handsome staff-quarters, with the houses of Governor and Lieutenant-Governor, beyond which are barracks of stone for 1,600 men and an artillery unit. It all has a slightly Adam touch in some of the detail, and William Adam, father of Robert, was in fact the contractor, but the design was not his but William Skinner's. The fortress was 21 years in the building, and in the end cost something approaching £200,000. The chapel, beyond the clock-tower block, was one of the last buildings completed, and the interior of this with its arcade and gallery supported on Doric columns, is quite delightful. Finally, in the staff-block, is the museum of the Queen's Own Highlanders. Beautifully laid out in an eighteenth century house of great charm, it covers the history of a regiment which combines the Seaforth and the Cameron Highlanders, and its uniforms, medals, weapons and musical instruments are enhanced by numerous pictures of the campaigns in which they were involved, including a painting of remarkable talent by a corporal of the regiment. There is a roomful of uniforms worn by members of the Royal Family over several generations, among them a series which belonged to King Edward VIII. Fort George is no longer a regimental depot, but is still used by territorials. Its sole remaining armaments are two grim 13-inch mortars positioned on the bastions, Victorian replacements of eighteenth-century mortars of similar type.

The other great early example of a public work on the grand scale in the vicinity of Inverness was also built with a military purpose, yet like Fort George had little or no direct involvement in war. It is, of course, the Caledonian Canal. Two-thirds of the canal consists of lochs, and the most evident section of the canal proper is between Douchfour at the head of Loch Ness and Clachnaharry, where the lochs connect with the Beauly Firth. Looked at from here, the canal is not an obviously formidable undertaking, and it might be wondered why it took from 1803 until 1847 to complete the work, or why it cost the then enormous sum of £1,300,000. The delay was partly due to the victory of Trafalgar, for the threat of French privateers round our coasts had been a main reason for projecting the scheme; but the problems facing the engineers were much less easily overcome than a first glance at the chain of big, deep lochs filling most of the Great Glen might have encouraged them to think. The levels of Loch Ness and Loch Lochy had to be raised substantially, 28 locks were required, and the canal was designed by Thomas Telford to take a 32-gun frigate. And there were unforeseen problems, such as the clearance from Loch Oich, highest of the chain of lochs, of an accumulation of enormous ancient oaks. The first traverse of the canal was actually in 1822, by a steam barge which went from Inverness to Fort William in 13 hours, but two days was reckoned goodtime for a passage by sail. It is not quite true to say the canal had no involvement in war, because it did have its uses for small vessels in both World Wars, but much of its earlier traffic was between North America and Baltic ports. To-day its most practical use is by fishing-boats moving between the east coast ports and the west, but it is also a pleasant and leisurely way of viewing some impressive scenery.

For decades past, tourists coming to the Great Glen have had eyes for little but a possible glimpse of the monster, yet Loch Ness and its neigbbourhood are packed with interest, both scenic and historic. For a start, this deep, straight valley, cutting Scotland in two, to use Geikie's words, offers a dramatic example of a geological fracture on a giant scale; but other forces have been at work here, and Geikie also pointed out that in the Ice Ages the glaciers which descended into this glen were more vast than anywhere else in Scotland, and that their striations prove that the lochs Ness, Oich and Lochy are not merely water lodging in a primeval fissure but in basins excavated by those enormous glaciers. Their mass and power are seen in the depth of Loch Ness, deeper by far than the North Sea, deeper even than the Atlantic for a considerable distance beyond the Outer Hebrides. At such depths the temperature is fairly constant, in Loch Ness about 42 degrees

Fahrenheit, and I believe that in sub-zero air temperatures the River Ness may steam, although I have never seen it. I seem to recall that this warmth of water and the possible existence of deep caverns linking with the sea have been offered as part explanations for the existence of a monster in the loch, but it must be remembered that in such a situation water-depths of such profundity are unaffected by wave action and are unaerated, and must be a rather hostile environment for any normal form of life. By contrast with such dark submarine chasms, the watershed in the glen is not much more than a hundred feet above sea-level. So imperceptible is it where it occurs between Loch Lochy and Loch Oich that a story is recorded of an old lady who lived here on the boundary which divided Lochiel's lands from Glengarry's evading her taxes regularly by diverting the boundary stream one way or another according to which factor was due to call! Pennant in the eighteenth century has nothing to say about monsters in Loch Ness, but he does note a more than usually violent example of the seismic disturbances which still occasionally trouble the line of the fault. On 1 November 1755, the time of the big Lisbon earthquake, he says the waters of Loch Ness 'rose and flowed up the lake from east to west with vast impetuosity ... continuing ebbing and flowing for the space of an hour; but at eleven o'clock a wave greater than any of the rest came up the river, broke on the north side and overflowed the bank for the extent of 30 feet.'

To the east of the Great Glen is a huge area which sees relatively few visitors. Its roads are few and are confined to the country near Loch Ness. Most of the area is occupied by the Monadhliath. Because the Monadhliath are not famous climbing grounds like the Cairngorms or Glencoe as hills they do not attract the dedicated mountaineers, and because their skylines are undramatic they seem to offer no objectives for the tourist and tend to be dismissed as rather desolate; but in fact they are a splendid region for the hill-walker. They are perhaps most easily penetrated by following the Findhorn up from Findhorn Bridge below Tomatin on the Great North Road. There is a road and then a track far up its left bank into Coignafearn Forest, around which there is a congregation of considerable summits, their names prefixed not by

196

Ben but usually by Carn, several of them exceeding 3,000 feet and therefore qualifying as Munros. This is a lonely country of magnificent distant views, a country of schistose rocks – Monadhliath means grey mountains – ground down by glacial action, but its very loneliness has made it a home for some of the rarer animals and birds: the wildcat, for instance, and the eagle and the ptarmigan. It is crossed at its southern end by a famous drove-road, which follows the headwaters of the Spey up over the Corrieyairack Pass, then down Glen Tarff to Fort Augustus. Wade's soldiers made a road over the Pass, and Charles Edward crossed it at the outset of his adventure, Johnny Cope withdrawing before him towards Ruthven Barracks, by no means an abject decision, because not only was his force inferior in strength and probably also in quality, but he also realised that in a mountain defile as menacing as the Corrieyairack even the best troops might have been no match for the clansmen. Some complain that Wade's road across this spectacular pass – it rises to 2,507 feet – should have been maintained and even developed for motor traffic, but to my mind the real wildernesses in Scotland now are all too few, and some objectives should be left that demand an effort to attain. The region closer to Loch Ness is well enough served by roads. A signpost just before the sharp bend of the Great North Road at Daviot points to Fort Augustus, and if one follows it the next hour or so is rewarding. The route follows Strath Nairn, close to a high moorland, remote and laced with lochs, the largest of them Duntelchaig, now harnessed as a reservoir for Inverness. A little way on Strath Nairn gives place to Strath Errick, and the road follows the shore of Loch Mhor to the village of Bailebeag, where there is a diversion to Foyers. Foyers is celebrated for its magnificent waterfalls, which have impressed many travellers, Pennant and Dr Johnson among them, the latter at one point averting his eyes from the 'dreadful depth'. Robert Burns was essentially a man of the Lowlands, but he too wrote of these 'mossy floods'. In 1894 it was decided to use the great head of water to generate electricity for an aluminium processing plant, the first hydro-electric installation in Scotland, but this comparatively small enterprise was later over-shadowed by the much larger plants at

Kinlochleven and Lochaber and eventually was closed down, although not before becoming a target for a German bomber in the Second War. Although the falls have never been restored to their former splendour, the country around is still beautiful. It is Fraser country. James Fraser of Foyers, like Cluny Macpherson, had to hide in a cave for long after the 'Forty-five, and many stories are told of his escapes from the Redcoats.

It seems to have been a superstitious Fraser who deprived Fort Augustus, at the south end of Loch Ness, of an ancient and significant relic. In 1559 old Lady Lovat went on a pilgrimage to the spot between Loch Oich and Loch Lochy where the Frasers and the Clanranald Macdonalds had fought the bloody 'Battle of the Shirts' fifteen years before, since she had lost her son and her husband there. She decided to take back with her the holy bell of St Cummin, preserved at Cille-Cumein, the village now called Fort Augustus, no doubt a Celtic bell similar to the bell of St Eunan at Kincraig, already mentioned. She and her party were being rowed homewards on Loch Ness, when one of the sudden fierce storms to which the loch is subject occurred and a Fraser oarsman advised the waters be placated by the sacrifice of the bell. Cille Cumein means 'church of Cummin', and St Cummin was one of Columba's successors in the abbacy of Iona. Columba himself used the Great Glen in pursuing his mission to the Picts, and Cummin clearly founded his seat on the route. It was in a strategic position at a point where the clans to the east of the loch, notably the Frasers, were bound to be constantly confronted by the powerful clans to the west, and a fort or castle of some kind was built there; and when Wade undertook his 'pacification' after the 'Fifteen he recognised the importance of the place and put up another fort close to an existing fortress-barracks on the point of land which divides the mouths of the small rivers Oich and Tarff. This fort fell easily to the Jacobites. Later, a final insult to the Highlanders, it was renamed Fort Augustus in honour of the Butcher Cumberland. Cumberland had his quarters here for a time and added to his notoriety, for when young Roderick Mackenzie was murdered by soldiers at Glenmoriston because of his close likeness to the Prince, and died deliberately claiming to be Charles Edward, his bleeding head was received with satisfaction at Fort Augustus by Cumberland himself, who went so far as to take it with him to London. Now what remains of the fort has been incorporated in the Benedictine abbey. This is just a century old, founded in 1876 by some monks from the *Schottenkloster* at Regensburg, a monastery which owes its name not to Scottish missionaries, as the name might suggest, but to Irish ones – the Scotti, of course, anciently being a tribe of Irish Dalriada. The abbey incorporates a public school for boys. Since changing place-names on our maps, and indeed resuscitating old names, is currently so acceptable, might I recommend to the new regional authority in the Highlands or to whomever it may concern, that the evil memory of Cumberland be expunged from the Great Glen by restoring the old name for this village, so much more meaningful than the present one. If Cille Cumein seems too unfamiliar, why not the once widely-used Kilcumein?

The east shores of Loch Ness and Loch Lochy are the extreme bounds of the Central Highland or Grampian region, however elastic one makes those bounds. Certainly they cannot be carried far up the long glens which penetrate the hills west of the two lochs. The Great Glen, however, has two sides to it like other glens, and the life and character of it are not entirely split by the deep waters which separate them, so that perhaps a brief trespass on the west shores is justified. To me, those shores are a sort of frontier behind which the real *Gaidhealtachd* has withdrawn. Wade and the Hanoverians recognised this when they put their chain of defences along this line, but a succession of remarkable men kept arising along the frontier to inspire now fear, now reluctant admiration and finally a mixture of exasperation and affection in the rest of the country. Like so many other Celts over a span of 2,000 years they would not admit defeat and never knew when they were beaten.

The home of the first of them was at Achnacarry, near the south end of Loch Lochy. It is the seat of Cameron of Lochiel. The present house is a successor to the castle destroyed by Cumberland after Culloden. There were many doughty holders of the name of Lochiel, and the great claymore of Allen Cameron, dated 1588, which is at Achnacarry is a symbol of their prowess as are the claymores carved on the gravestones of many other West Highland chieftains. But he who is best remembered is Donald, the 19th Chief, who was called the Gentle Lochiel. He was the embodiment of the ancient Celt. Well aware of the unwisdom of this Jacobite adventure, he did all he could to presuade Charles Edward to abandon it, but when the Prince taunted him with cowardice he threw all caution to the winds, rallied his clansmen even to threatening them with fire and sword if they did not follow him in the cause of the *Ard Righ,* their rightful king, and abandoned for ever his peaceful ploy of beautifying the policies of Achnacarry. There is a stand of great trees near the house which is said to have come from a row of seedlings hastily heeled into a trench to await Lochiel's return, in vain. At Culloden he led his men on to the guns until he fell, his ankles shattered by grapeshot. He was carried from the field and went into hiding, later to watch his own house put to the flames. At last he escaped to France, and there he died two years after the battle. It is believed that 37,000 loius d'or, brought by French vessels to help continue the rebellion, are hid in seven barrels sunk in Loch Arkaig behind Achnacarry – one of those treasure tales which is perhaps better founded than most.

Some miles northwards the Great Glen passes into Macdonald country. Between Loch Lochy and Loch Oich was fought the Battle of the Shirts referred to earlier in the matter of the bell of St Cummin. It was a famous fight, if creditable to no one, an extreme case of those clan feuds which were carried on with such ferocity, and it came by its name because in the extreme heat of a July day both sides threw off their plaids and fought in kilt and shirt. A curious monument beside Loch Oich, a sort of incurving obelisk on a square base, topped by a finial carved in a cluster of seven heads, commemorates another bloodthirsty clan incident. It is called *Tobar-nan-ceann,* Well of the Heads, and the story behind it is that Macdonald of Keppoch in the seventeenth century sent his two sons to be educated abroad, but died in their absence, and when they returned his seven brothers murdered them, apparently because they resented the new young chief's notions about putting down lawlessness. A party of the Macdonalds of Sleat was guided by Ian Lom, famed as a bard and still so famed, to the house where the murderers were asleep and the seven were despatched and their

200

heads laid before the chief, Glengarry, with the taunt from Ian Lom
that he should not have left the job to his kinsmen from the Isles.
First the bard washed the heads in a spring, and it is this spring
over which the little monument was raised generations later, in
1812 by Colonel Alastair Macdonell, last Chief of Glengarry. This
Glengarry was a man born out of his time. A grand-nephew of
Alastair Ruadh Macdonell, otherwise Roderick Random and
Pickle the Spy, he was spontaneous and colourful and beloved by
many. Sir Walter Scott, to whom he gave the deerhound Maida
which lies at Scott's feet in more than one picture, called him a
treasure and put him in *Waverley* in the character of Fergus
MacIvor. He was also, however, the traditional Highland hot-head.
When he raised the Glengarry Fencibles on his estates he turned
out of his house any man who disobeyed the order to join simply
because he had refused to serve his chief, and when he travelled it
was with his 'arms and his tail' – his weapons and his armed
retinue – in the ancient manner, even in the State Procession when
George IV visited Edinburgh. He constantly brought trouble on
himself. The most famous example began at a ball at Inverness,
when a young Lieutenant Macleod of the 42nd, a grandson of Flora
herself, had the temerity to secure a dance from the belle of the ball,
Miss Forbes of Culloden, to whom Glengarry had been paying 'a
deal of attention'. Glengarry picked a quarrel with Macleod,
challenged him and slew him in the duel. On the advice of his
counsel, Henry Erskine, he surrendered himself to the authorities
and was tried for murder in the High Court in Edinburgh before
Lord Eskgrove – Roughead in his account of the trial records that
the Lord Justice-Clerk, Braxfield, was in his last illness, which was
perhaps as well for Glengarry. The accused was acquitted, but
Erskine, his counsel, refused to attend the dinner to celebrate the
verdict. The portrait of Glengarry by Raeburn in the National
Gallery of Scotland is typical of the man, and Raeburn obviously
relished painting it. The picture bristles with weapons – targe and
broadswords on the wall behind, a gun in the Chief's hand, a pistol
protruding from his belt, a superb ivory-hilted dirk at his side.
About forty years ago on a grey winter day I was visiting a house in
the old village of Culross in Fife when my hostess put before me the

weapons of Glengarry, the very weapons which Raeburn had painted. They were magnificent examples not so much of the true ancient Highland arms, but of the costume pieces after the old style which those who could afford them commissioned to be made in the romantic days of Scott, the best-known instances of which are probably the Clanranald pistols now in the National Museum of Antiquities in Edinburgh. And those who could afford them certainly did not include Alastair Macdonell of Glengarry. When he died in 1928, his clansmen insisted on their right to carry Mac-Mhic-Alastair shoulder high and they streamed to his castle from every glen, and with flaming torches and the Chief's piper the procession went on its way through a thunderstorm to Kilfinnan, the clansmen at the last having to carry their burden through a stream swollen by the storm; but after it was over Glengarry's estates had to be sold to pay his debts, and his son and heir had to emigrate to Australia. All that is left is the ruined castle upon Creag an Fhitheach, the Rock of the Raven, on the shore of Loch Oich. 'Creag an Fhitheach' was the war-cry of the Macdonells of Glengarry. It is perhaps an appropriate note on which to end.

Index

Index

Index